The Complete AT Study Guide

WAVE

★
™

THOMSON LEARNING

APLS-SGMN-1021A

Contents

Contents

Foreword

This study guide is designed to help experienced candidates prepare for exams. The modules in the study guide are targeted to specific test objectives.

The material in the study guide focuses directly on the exam criteria. Background information, examples, and similar aids are not included in the study guide modules. The materials assume that you are already familiar with the materials and are using the study guide as a quick review before taking the exam.

While it can be used by itself as a preparation tool, the study guide is designed as part of a suite of training materials including self-study manuals, video segments, and practice exams. It is strongly suggested that less experienced learners make use of all of these materials when preparing for an examination. More experienced learners will find that their performance on the examinations will improve if they take advantage of all of the available materials.

As reinforcement and review for certification exams, study guides are particularly effective with the *Challenge! Interactive™*. The *Challenge!* contains sample test items for the exams. The sample tests are comprised of multiple-choice, screen simulation, and scenario questions to better prepare you for exams. It is a good idea to take the *Challenge!* test on a particular exam, read the study guide, and then take the *Challenge!* test again. It is useful to take the *Challenge!* tests as frequently as possible because they are excellent reinforcement tools.

Foreword

This study guide is designed to help experienced candidates prepare for exams. The modules in the study guide are targeted to specific test objectives.

The material in the study guide focuses directly on the exam content. Background information, examples, and similar aids are not included in the study guide modules. The content assumes that you are already familiar with the materials and are using the study guide as a quick review before taking the exam.

Exam Criteria Matrices

EXAM 220-201: A+ CORE HARDWARE

The following table maps the course materials to each of the exam objective topics. Criteria specific to each topic is listed as well as a reference to the specific area in *A+ Core Hardware* and media that cover it.

For the most current test objectives, access the following Web site:

http://www.comptia.com/certification/

NOTE: *The criteria have been numbered to facilitate cross-referencing between the matrix and the modules. This is not necessarily the numbering scheme of the certifying agency.*

Topic	Criteria	Course Manual	Multiple-Media Resources
Domain 1.0 Installation, Configuration, and Upgrading	1.1 Identify basic terms, concepts, and functions of system modules, including how each module should work during normal operation and during the boot process.	Chapter 1 • Basic Functions Chapter 3 Chapter 4 Chapter 5	**Digital Video** • Touring the Inside of a PC • Installing Components **Challenge! Interactive** • Installation, Configuration, and Upgrading
	1.2 Identify basic procedures for adding and removing field replaceable modules for both desktop and portable systems.	Chapter 3 • Laptops Chapter 7 Chapter 8 • Power Supplies	**Digital Video** • Touring the Inside of a PC • Installing Components **Challenge! Interactive** • Installation, Configuration, and Upgrading
	1.3 Identify available IRQs, DMAs, and I/O addresses and procedures for configuring them for device installation and configuration.	Chapter 7	**Challenge! Interactive** • Installation, Configuration, and Upgrading

Topic	Criteria	Course Manual	Multiple-Media Resources
Domain 1.0 Installation, Configuration, and Upgrading	1.4 Identify common peripheral ports, associated cabling, and their connectors.	*Chapter 5* *Chapter 13*	***Challenge! Interactive*** • Installation, Configuration, and Upgrading
	1.5 Identify proper procedures for installing and configuring IDE/EIDE devices.	*Chapter 7* • Installing a Disk Drive Adapter • Hard Disk Installation	***Challenge! Interactive*** • Installation, Configuration, and Upgrading
	1.6 Identify proper procedures for installing and configuring SCSI devices.	*Chapter 7* • Hard Disk Installation	***Challenge! Interactive*** • Installation, Configuration, and Upgrading
	1.7 Identify proper procedures for installing and configuring peripheral devices.	*Chapter 3* *Chapter 7*	**Digital Video** • Touring the Inside of a PC • Installing Components ***Challenge! Interactive*** • Installation, Configuration, and Upgrading
	1.8 Identify hardware methods of upgrading system performance, procedures for replacing basic subsystem components, and unique components and when to use them.	*Chapter 7* • Installing a Disk Drive Adapter • Hard Disk Installation	***Challenge! Interactive*** • Installation, Configuration, and Upgrading
Domain 2.0 Diagnosing and Troubleshooting	2.1 Identify common symptoms and problems associated with each module and how to troubleshoot and isolate the problems.	*Chapter 8*	***Challenge! Interactive*** • Diagnosing and Troubleshooting
	2.2 Identify basic troubleshooting procedures and how to elicit problem symptoms from customers.	*Chapter 6*	***Challenge! Interactive*** • Diagnosing and Troubleshooting

Topic	Criteria	Course Manual	Multiple-Media Resources
Domain 3.0 Safety and Preventive Maintenance	3.1 Identify the purpose of various types of preventive maintenance products and procedures and when to use and perform them.	*Chapter 6* • Ongoing Maintenance	***Challenge! Interactive*** • Safety and Preventive Maintenance
	3.2 Identify issues, procedures, and devices for protection within the computing environment, including people, hardware, and the surrounding workspace.	*Chapter 2*	***Challenge! Interactive*** • Safety and Preventive Maintenance
Domain 4.0 Motherboard/ Processors/ Memory	4.1 Distinguish between the popular CPU chips in terms of their basic characteristics.	*Chapter 3* • Microprocessors	**Digital Video** • Touring the Inside of a PC • Installing Components ***Challenge! Interactive*** • Motherboard/Processors/ Memory
	4.2 Identify the categories of RAM (Random Access Memory) terminology, their locations, and physical characteristics.	*Chapter 3* • System Memory • Laptop Components	**Digital Video** • Touring the Inside of a PC • Installing Components ***Challenge! Interactive*** • Motherboard/Processors/ Memory
	4.3 Identify the most popular type of motherboards, their components, and their architecture (bus structures and power supplies).	*Chapter 3* • System Boards • Expansion Bus *Chapter 5* *Chapter 7* • System Board Configuration	**Digital Video** • Touring the Inside of a PC • Installing Components ***Challenge! Interactive*** • Motherboard/Processors/ Memory
	4.4 Identify the purpose of CMOS (Complementary Metal Oxide Semiconductor), what it contains, and how to change its basic parameters.	*Chapter 7* • CMOS	***Challenge! Interactive*** • Motherboard/Processors/ Memory

Topic	Criteria	Course Manual	Multiple-Media Resources
Domain 5.0 Printers	5.1 Identify basic concepts, printer operations, and printer components.	*Chapter 9*	***Challenge! Interactive*** • Printers
	5.2 Identify care and service techniques and common problems with primary printer types.	*Chapter 2* • Potential Hazards with Computer Equipment • Potential Hazards to Computer Equipment *Chapter 10*	***Challenge! Interactive*** • Printers
Domain 6.0 Basic Networking	6.1 Identify basic networking concepts, including how a network works and the ramifications of repairs on the network.	*Chapter 11* *Chapter 12* *Chapter 13*	**Digital Video** • Networking Fundamentals • The OSI Model ***Challenge! Interactive*** • Basic Networking

EXAM 220-202: A+ OPERATING SYSTEM (OS) TECHNOLOGIES

The following table maps the course materials to each of the exam objective topics. Criteria specific to each topic is listed as well as a reference to the specific area in *A+ Operating Systems (OS)* and media that cover it.

For the most current test objectives, access the following Web site:

http://www.comptia.com/certification/

NOTE: *The criteria have been numbered to facilitate cross-referencing between the matrix and the modules. This is not necessarily the numbering scheme of the certifying agency.*

Topic	Criteria	Course Manual	Multiple-Media Resources

Domain 1.0 OS Fundamentals	1.1 Identify the operating system's functions, structure, and major system files to navigate the operating system and how to get to needed technical information.	*Chapter 1*
		Chapter 4
		• Windows 95/98 System Files
		• Windows 2000 System Files
		• Navigating Windows 95/98
		Chapter 5
		• The FAT32 File System
		Chapter 7
		• Memory Fundamentals
		• Windows 98 Memory Management
		Chapter 8
		• DOS Commands
			Digital Video
			• Navigating Windows 98
			• Navigating Windows 2000
			NEXTSim
			• Operating System Orientation
			  ○ Create a Shortcut to a Network Server
			  ○ Use Windows Explorer to Find a File
			  ○ Change the Folder Options to Show All Files
			  ○ Customize the Start Menu
			• Software Management
			  ○ Use the Command Prompt to Manage Files and Directories
			Challenge! Interactive
			• OS Fundamentals

Topic	Criteria	Course Manual	Multiple-Media Resources

Domain 1.0 OS Fundamentals	1.2 Identify basic concepts and procedures for creating, viewing, and managing files, directories, and disks. This includes procedures for changing file attributes and the ramifications of those changes (for example, security issues).	*Chapter 5*
		• The FAT32 File System
		• Hard Drive Optimization
		• Using Microsoft Backup for Windows 98
		Chapter 6
		• Using Windows 2000 Backup Utility
		• Using Encrypting File System
		• Managing Data Compression
			NEXTSim
			• Windows 98 Disk and File Management
			  ○ Convert FAT16 Drive to FAT32 Using Drive Converter
			  ○ Run System Utilities for Hard Disk Management
			  ○ Install and Use Microsoft Backup
			• Windows 2000 Disk and File Management
			  ○ Use Microsoft Backup to Back Up Files
			  ○ Encrypt Files
			Challenge! Interactive
			• OS Fundamentals

	1.3 Identify the procedures for basic disk management.	*Chapter 5*
		Chapter 6
			NEXTSim
			• Windows 98 Disk and File Management
			  ○ Run System Utilities for Hard Disk Management
			  ○ Schedule Tasks in Windows 98
			  ○ Install and Use Microsoft Backup
			• Windows 2000 Disk and File Management
			  ○ Use Microsoft Backup to Back Up Files
			  ○ Use Microsoft Backup to Restore Files
			Challenge! Interactive
			• OS Fundamentals

Topic	Criteria	Course Manual	Multiple-Media Resources
Domain 2.0 Installation, Configuration, and Upgrading	2.1 Identify the procedures for installing Windows 9x and Windows 2000 for bringing the software to a basic operational level.	*Chapter 2* *Chapter 3*	**Digital Video** • Windows 98 Installation • Windows 2000 Installation **NEXTSim** • Windows 95/98 Installation ○ Upgrade Windows 95 to Windows 98 ***Challenge! Interactive*** • Installation, Configuration, and Upgrading
	2.2 Identify steps to perform an operating system upgrade.	*Chapter 2* *Chapter 3*	**Digital Video** • Windows 98 Installation • Windows 2000 Installation **NEXTSim** • Windows 95/98 Installation ○ Upgrade Windows 95 to Windows 98 ***Challenge! Interactive*** • Installation, Configuration, and Upgrading

Topic	Criteria	Course Manual	Multiple-Media Resources
Domain 2.0 Installation, Configuration, and Upgrading	2.3 Identify the basic system boot sequences and boot methods, including the steps to create an emergency boot disk with utilities installed for Windows 9x, Windows NT, and Windows 2000.	*Chapter 2* *Chapter 4* • Windows 95/98 Boot Process • Windows 2000 Boot Process • Boot Diskettes	**Digital Video** • Windows 98 Installation • Navigating Windows 98 • Navigating Windows 2000 **NEXTSim** • Windows 95/98 Installation ○ Upgrade Windows 95 to Windows 98 ***Challenge! Interactive*** • Installation, Configuration, and Upgrading

	2.4 Identify procedures for loading/adding and configuring application device drivers and the necessary software for certain devices.	*Chapter 7*
		 • Device Drivers
		 • Windows 2000 Device Drivers
		 • Windows 98 Printer Management
		 Chapter 8
		 • Microsoft Windows Application Support
		 • 16-Bit and 32-Bit Windows Applications
		 Chapter 10
		 • Resource Sharing
			NEXTSim
			 • Hardware Management
			   ○ Configure and Troubleshoot an I/O Device
			   ○ Configure Printing
			 • Software Management
			   ○ Configure a DOS-based Application
			
			 Challenge! Interactive
			 • Installation, Configuration, and Upgrading

Topic	Criteria	Course Manual	Multiple-Media Resources

Domain 3.0 Diagnosing and Troubleshooting	3.1 Recognize and interpret the meaning of common error codes and startup messages from the boot sequence and identify steps to correct the problems.	*Chapter 4*
		 • Windows 2000 System Files
		 Chapter 7
		 • Memory Fundamentals
		 • Windows 98 Memory Management
		 • Device Drivers
		 Chapter 8
		 • Windows Error Messages
		 Chapter 12
			Digital Video
			 • Navigating Windows 98
			 • Navigating Windows 2000
			 • Windows 98 Troubleshooting Tools
			 • Windows 2000 Troubleshooting Tools
			 NEXTSim
			 • Hardware Management
			    ○ Configure and Troubleshoot an I/O Device
			 • Software Management
			    ○ Modify Dr. Watson Options in Windows 2000
			 • Troubleshooting Windows
			    ○ Use System Configuration Utility and Sysedit
			    ○ Create and Configure an Alert Object
			    ○ Use the Event Viewer
			 Challenge! Interactive
			 • Diagnosing and Troubleshooting

Topic	Criteria	Course Manual	Multiple-Media Resources

Domain 3.0 Diagnosing and Troubleshooting	3.2 Recognize common problems and determine how to resolve them.	*Chapter 4*
		• Windows 95/98 System Files
		• Windows 2000 System Files
		Chapter 5
		• Hard Drive Optimization
		Chapter 8
		• Windows Error Messages
		• Virus Prevention
		Chapter 12
			Digital Video
			• Navigating Windows 98
			• Navigating Windows 2000
			• Windows 98 Troubleshooting Tools
			• Windows 2000 Troubleshooting Tools
			NEXTSim
			• Windows 98 Disk and File Management
			  ○ Run System Utilities for Hard Disk Management
			• Software Management
			  ○ Modify Dr. Watson Options in Windows 2000
			• Troubleshooting Windows
			  ○ Create and Configure an Alert Object
			  ○ Use the Event Viewer
			Challenge! Interactive
			• Diagnosing and Troubleshooting

Topic	Criteria	Course Manual	Multiple-Media Resources

Domain 4.0 Networks	4.1 Identify the networking capabilities of Windows, including procedures for connecting to the network.	*Chapter 9*
		Chapter 10
		Chapter 11
			NEXTSim
			• Windows 98 LAN Management
			  ○ Network and Share Resources on Windows 98
			  ○ Share Folders with a NetWare Network
			• Internet Technologies
			  ○ Create a Dial-up Networking Connection in Windows 98
			  ○ Install the Internet Connection Sharing Utility in Windows 98
			  ○ Configure or Troubleshoot a Modem
			  ○ Connect to the Internet Using Dial-up Networking
			Challenge! Interactive
			• **Networks**

Topic	Criteria	Course Manual	Multiple-Media Resources

Domain 4.0 Networks	4.2 Identify concepts and capabilities relating to the Internet and basic procedures for setting up a system for Internet access.	*Chapter 9*
		Chapter 11
			NEXTSim
			• Windows 98 LAN Management
			  o Network a Windows 98 Computer to a NetWare Server
			  o Network a Windows 98 Computer to a Windows NT Server
			• Internet Technologies
			  o Create a Dial-up Networking Connection in Windows 98
			  o Install the Internet Connection Sharing Utility in Windows 98
			  o Connect to the Internet Using Dial-up Networking
			Challenge! Interactive
			• Networks

Module 1
Exam 220-201: A+ Core Hardware

DOMAIN 1.0 INSTALLATION, CONFIGURATION, AND UPGRADING

Exam Criteria

1.1 Identify basic terms, concepts, and functions of system modules, including how each module should work during normal operation and during the boot process.

Points to Remember

Basic Functions

- Input
  - It is the way that the user enters information into the computer.
  - Input devices include a keyboard, mouse, and modem.
- Processing

  Once data is inputted, it performs specific instructions on the data.
- Output
  - An output device provides an interface between the computer and the user.
  - Output devices include monitors, printers, and modems.
- Storage
  - It provides a way for the user to record data.
  - Data is magnetically recorded onto storage devices, such as hard disks, floppy disks, and tapes.

System Modules

- Power supplies
  - A device is required to convert the power from the wall socket to the power required by the computer.
  - AT power supplies

    Two 6-pin connectors, typically labeled P8 and P9, to the motherboard, end to end with the black wire of each connector side by side
  - ATX power supplies
    - One 20-pin connector connects to the system board called a Molex connector.
    - An ATX power supply routes the on/off switch through the system board.
  - Standard features
    - Power supplies have multiple internal connectors called *power connectors* that are used to connect power to peripherals.
    - The most common rating for power supplies is in *watts*.
    - AC is converted to DC in the power supply. There are four voltages present in a power supply: +12 volts, -12 volts, +5 volts, and -5 volts.
- System boards
  - They are also called motherboards, mainboards, and planar boards.
  - It provides support for all the components installed on the board.
  - Performance issues
    - Speed

      Processor's clock speed, size of its internal and external data buses, processor design, supporting chipset
    - Configuration
    - Memory

      Amount and type of memory
    - Bus type

      AGP, PCI, or ISA

- Supporting chipset circuitry

  Interfaces between PC's subsystems

  - Software support

  o ATX motherboard

  - 90-degree rotation of expansion and microprocessor slots

  - New layout providing more space for full-length add-in cards

  - New layout requiring fewer cables

  - New layout providing better cooling and ventilation

  - Lower manufacturing costs

- Microprocessor/CPU

  o Considered the computer's *brain*

  o Floating Point Unit (FPU)

  Sometimes referred to as a math coprocessor

  o Processor performance

  - The internal clock speed, measured in megahertz, is the speed at which the processor obtains information within its own confines.

  - The external clock speed is the speed at which the processor accesses information outside itself in external cache memory or system RAM.

  o Internal cache memory

  Cache memory is a very fast memory that keeps a copy of frequently used data and instructions.

- Firmware

  o Basic Input and Output System (BIOS)

  - BIOS contains all of the software required to control the basic functions of the system board.

  - A Flash BIOS can be periodically updated with new software to fix bugs and add support for new technologies.

  o Complementary Metal Oxide Semiconductor (CMOS)

  Configuration information is stored in CMOS RAM and is maintained by a battery.

- System memory
  - o Random Access Memory (RAM) is for short-term storage of data and programs and is volatile, meaning that the information is lost if the system is powered down or restarted.
  - o Read Only Memory (ROM) is nonvolatile memory, meaning that the contents of memory are retained even when system power is shut off.
- Storage
  - o Hard disk drives
    - The primary device used for mass storage is the hard disk.
    - Data is written onto the platters or read from them by read/write heads, which can access both sides of the platters.
  - o Removable media drives
    - Floppy disk drives
      - o A floppy is the first method of storage before the hard drive.
      - o They work in a fashion similar to hard drives except the read/write head actually touches the disk.
    - CD-ROMs
      - o These are used for data distribution, such as for large look-up libraries, software manuals, and large applications that require CD-ROM capacity (up to 650 MB per CD) to install.
      - o Digital data is written to the discs using special recording equipment that makes microscopic pits in the disc surface and is read by detecting changes in reflectivity using a photodetector.
    - Digital Video Disc (DVD)
      - o DVDs provide digital information on discs the size and shape of audio CDs.
      - o Capacity of each DVD is 4.7 GB.
    - Zip drives
      - o The most successful removable storage system on the market, it weighs less than 2 pounds, and the discs hold 100 or 250 MB of information.
      - o They use either parallel or SCSI connectors.

- Monitors

  The monitor, or Cathode Ray Tube (CRT), is a vacuum tube that houses a flat screen coated with Phosphors at one end and an electron gun at the other.

  o   Phosphors glow when the electron beam hits them, producing a bright spot at the point of impact.

  o   The actual dots of created light are called pixels and are actually made up of three phosphors representing the primary colors: red, green, and blue.

  o   The electrons strike only the intended phosphor color on each pixel with different intensities and angles to achieve the desired color.

- Laptop displays

  o   Laptop and notebook computers use Liquid Crystal Display (LCD) technology.

  o   Liquid crystals are manipulated by charged vertical and horizontal wires that create pixels where the lines intersect.

  o   Passive matrix

      As the electrical charge moves away from the intersection and continues down the wire, the pixel begins to fade as the crystal loses its electrical energy.

  o   Active matrix

      The electrical charge that simulates the crystal is regulated by a Thin Film Transistor (TFT) that uses a capacitor to provide the crystal with the appropriate current to remain in its excited state.

- System ports

  o   Serial port

      - Bits of information are sent in a *series,* one at a time, in a straight line.

      - It supports 9- or 25-pin D connectors.

  o   Parallel port (LPT port)

      - Eight data bits are sent in *parallel,* all at the same time.

      - It uses a 25-pin D-shell (Centronics) connector.

      - Cables for the IEEE 1284 standard support a higher data transfer rate than Centronics.

- ○ Universal Serial Bus (USB) ports

  Rectangular shape

- ○ PS/2 ports

  These are sometimes color coded to make it easier to determine which port is for the keyboard and which is for the mouse.

- Modems
  - ○ The modem fulfills the role of Data Communication Equipment (DCE), linking Data Terminal Equipment (DTE).
  - ○ The word modem gets its definition from the tasks it performs. It acts as a *mo*dulator (digital to analog) and a *dem*odulator (analog to digital) when communicating with other computer systems across standard telephone lines.
  - ○ Internal modems require only a cable to connect the modem to the RJ-11 receptacle in the wall. An external modem will also require a serial or USB cable.
  - ○ Since there is no need to convert the digital signal to analog for transmission, ISDN modems are not a modulator/demodulator but more like a Network Interface Card (NIC).
  - ○ Cable modems connect a PC's Ethernet card to the coaxial TV cable.

Course Reference Material

Manual

- Chapter 1
  - ○ Basic Functions
- Chapter 3
- Chapter 4
- Chapter 5

Digital Video

- Touring the Inside of a PC
- Installing Components

Challenge! Interactive

- Installation, Configuration, and Upgrading

Exam Criteria

1.2   Identify basic procedures for adding and removing field replaceable modules for both desktop and portable systems.

Points to Remember

Field Replaceable Unit (FRU) Installation and Removal

- System board configuration
  - ○ Initial configuration

    System settings must be set to match any installed hardware.
  - ○ Routine reconfiguration

    Each time you make changes to configured devices or subsystems, it will be necessary to reconfigure your system to match.
  - ○ Battery replacement

    When the battery is replaced, setup information is lost and requires reconfiguration.
  - ○ ISA system configuration
    - System configuration parameters are stored in CMOS RAM.
    - During Startup, the configuration stored in CMOS is compared against what is sensed as being currently installed.
    - Common settings include time and date, system base, extended memory, number and type of floppy drives, number and type of hard disks, monitor type, and printer port type.
  - ○ Micro Channel Architecture (MCA) configuration
    - System reconfiguration is required any time changes are made to configured devices or when power is lost from the battery backup.
    - Configuration errors are reported to the screen during Startup as an error code of 16x.
    - To configure devices, you will need a *reference diskette*.
    - The **Configuration** menu will allow you to view the current configuration or to modify the configuration.

- o   EISA configuration

   After starting the system, you need to run the system Setup utility, or configuration utility, to configure the system.

- CPU (Central Processing Unit)

   - o   Before installing any new chip onto a motherboard, jumpers for CPU speed, clock multiplier, voltage, memory type, etc., must be set according to the motherboard's manufacturer specifications to match the processor being installed.

   - o   Low Insertion Force (LIF)

      - LIF requires a chip puller, a tool similar to a tiny crowbar used to pry the chip from its socket.

      - The chip is pried out alternately from one side, then the other, a little at a time using a rocking motion.

      - The replacement chip must be pushed straight down into the socket to avoid bending or breaking the pins.

      - Pin 1 was usually marked with a white dot, which was matched to a dot or notch on the socket.

   - o   Zero Insertion Force (ZIF)

      - ZIF has a levered arm that releases the chip when raised so that it can be effortlessly pulled out without damage.

      - The chip is replaced and the lever locked down into place.

      - Pin 1 is usually marked by a beveled corner matching a beveled corner in the socket so that the chip cannot be installed wrong.

      - If required, the heat sink sits directly over the installed chip and is held in place by a spring with clips at each end. A CPU fan may then be screwed in place over the heat sink and plugged to a power connection.

   - o   Single Edge Connector (SEC)

      - Pentium III heat sink and fan are installed to the unlabeled side of the processor before installation to the motherboard via two locking levers.

      - Celeron comes complete with the heat sink/fan already added; simply insert it into the SEC on the motherboard.

- Memory upgrade or replacement
  - ○ Single In-Line Memory Module (SIMM)
    - SIMMs must be replaced or added in banks.
    - The most common 72-pin bank layout is two SIMM strips per bank.
    - The most common 30-pin bank layout is four SIMM strips per bank.
    - The modules, which are keyed, are inserted into the open slot at an angle and then pushed upright where they will lock into place.
  - ○ Dual In-Line Memory Module (DIMM)
    - Currently all implementations of DIMM sockets use one DIMM socket per bank.
    - DIMMs slide directly downward into the slot and are locked into place at both ends by locking arms that swing upward over the notched ends.
  - ○ Rambus In-Line Memory Module (RIMM)

    The chips are covered by a form of heat sink called a *heat spreader*.

IDE Hard Disk Removal and Replacement

- Open the case and locate the hard disk drive.
- Locate the data cable and power cable and carefully remove them from the hard drive.
- Remove any screws that secure the drive to the computer and remove the hard drive.
- Reinstall the hard drive and carefully reconnect the cables.

Power Supply Installation

- AT power supplies
  - ○ The first step is to screw the power supply into place.
  - ○ Next, connect the power connectors, P8 and P9, so that the black wires face together to the system board.
  - ○ Connect the power switch to the front of the system case.
  - ○ The final step is to connect power to any drives in the system.

- ATX power supplies

  Installation of an ATX power supply is basically the same as installing an AT power supply except:

  o The single system board power connector is keyed, so it cannot be improperly connected.

  o The power switch is routed through the system board so there is no power switch to mount.

SCSI Tape Drive Installation

- If it is a SCSI device, and is configured using jumpers, configure the SCSI adapter card before installation.

- Open case, locate available slot, install SCSI adapter card, and close case.

- Connect the tape drive to the SCSI adapter and run the software configuration software if the card does not use jumpers.

- Install bundled backup program software.

Scanner Installation

- Connect scanner to the SCSI, parallel, or USB connector on the computer (depending on the type of scanner).

- Run the software installation program.

CD-ROM Installation

- Whether a SCSI or IDE device, the CD-ROM uses the same installation procedure as a corresponding hard drive.

- Once the data cable and power cable are connected, you will still need to connect the audio cable between the CD-ROM and the sound card in order to play CD sound through the system.

- Some early CD-ROMs were sold bundled with proprietary sound cards and have the IDE connector on the sound card itself. It is very important to make sure all drivers are available before removing and deleting drivers as they are not generally recognized as Plug and Play devices and drivers are difficult to get.

  If you have to replace the sound card on a bundled CD-ROM sound card combination, you generally will have to replace the CD-ROM as well because the data cable will not plug to a standard IDE port on a motherboard.

Connecting the Keyboard

- After turning off the system, plug in the keyboard and it is ready to use.
- AT keyboards use a 5-pin Deutsche Industrinorm (DIN) connector.
- ATX-based systems use a mini 6-pin DIN connector called a PS/2 connector.

Mouse Installation

Plug the mouse to an available serial, Universal Serial Bus (USB), or PS/2 mouse connector.

Expansion Card Installation

- Open the case and locate an expansion card of the right type–ISA, PCI, or AGP.
- Configure any jumpers or DIP switches on the cards.
- If there is a screw and baffle located at the back of the slot, remove them.
- Position the card into the slot and press it firmly into place.

Laptop Components

- Memory

  Small Outline Dual In-Line Memory Modules (SODIMMs) are usually installed directly underneath the keyboard or sometimes under a cover on the bottom of the laptop. The keyboard release varies by manufacturer, but the memory slides directly into a memory slot underneath.

- Hard disks

  Hard disks are either installed underneath the keyboard or under a cover on the bottom of the laptop. Simply boot the laptop after installation and configure in the BIOS if not autodetected.

- PC Cards

  These cards simply slide into the PC Card slot in the laptop and usually configure upon boot. PC Cards may be memory expansion cards, modems, SCSI, sound cards, network adapters, or hard drives. Some software installation may be necessary.

- AC adapters

  Simply plug these into the laptop in the appropriate connector. Some laptops have the DC converter built onto the wall socket connector, while others have DC adapters built internally into the laptop with the AC cable being nothing more than a power cable.

- Pointing devices
  - o Rollerball

    This is essentially an upside-down mouse ball built onto the body of the laptop between the right and left *mouse* buttons.
  - o Pointing stick

    This is a small rubber-tipped, eraser-shaped device that moves the cursor in a 360-degree motion using the same principles as a game joystick.
  - o Touchpad

    This is a flat pressure-sensitive panel that moves the cursor in concert with finger motion.
  - o External mouse

    An external mouse may be plugged into a laptop's serial, USB, or serial port if desired.

Course Reference Material

Manual

- Chapter 3
  - o Laptops
- Chapter 7
- Chapter 8
  - o Power Supplies

Digital Video

- Touring the Inside of a PC
- Installing Components

Challenge! Interactive

- Installation, Configuration, and Upgrading

Exam Criteria

1.3   Identify available IRQs, DMAs, and I/O addresses and procedures for configuring them for device installation and configuration.

Points to Remember

Interrupt Request (IRQ)

- The IRQ line is used to tell the processor when the board is requesting some type of service.
- The original IBM 8-bit system had eight IRQs; the AT 16-bit system added eight more.
- Each device has a unique IRQ value assigned.
- Some PCI cards may share an IRQ through PCI bridges.
- Common IRQs

0	System timer
1	Keyboard
2	Cascade from IRQ9
3	COM2, COM4, COM6, COM8
4	COM1, COM3, COM5, COM7
5	LPT2 (often available)
6	Floppy controller
7	LPT1
8	Real-time clock
9	VGA, NIC, software redirection to IRQ2 (INT 0Ah)
10	Available
11	Available
12	Available
13	Math coprocessor
14	Hard disk controller
15	Hard disk controller

Direct Memory Access (DMA)

- A DMA channel may be assigned to that board to allow it to communicate directly with system memory, bypassing the processor.
- The original IBM PC had four DMA channels; newer systems have eight.
- Common DMAs

0	Available (ISA/AT and above)
1	Hard disk controller, XT only (available for ISA/AT and above)
2	Floppy controller
3 to 7	Available

I/O Address

- It is a mapped memory area used to pass I/O commands to the boards and pass status information back to the processor.
- All addresses are in hexadecimal.
- It is necessary to assign an I/O address to most device controllers that you install in your system.

Memory Address

- This is the address assigned to ROM expansion memory that is physically located on expansion boards.
- These addresses are located in the area between 640 KB and 1,024 KB of system memory, the reserved or *high* memory area.

Addressing Configuration

- ISA 8- and 16-bit expansion boards are often configured through switch or jumper settings.
- In some instances, the configuration may be *hardwired*, or engineered into the board design, and cannot be changed.
- PCI boards are generally Plug and Play compatible and are automatically detected and configured by the system.
- Resources can be changed or assigned for Plug and Play systems through the hardware.

Course Reference Material

Manual

- Chapter 7

Challenge! Interactive

- Installation, Configuration, and Upgrading

Exam Criteria

1.4   Identify common peripheral ports, associated cabling, and their connectors.

Points to Remember

Internal Cables

- Ribbon cables
  - These are flat, gray cables that are used primarily for internal connections inside of a computer.
  - You must line up the Pin 1 red or blue stripe with Pin 1 on the interface and drive connectors or the device will not function.
- Integrated Drive Electronics (IDE) cables
  - These have three connectors: one to the motherboard and two for devices.
  - It may connect two devices to a cable at once as long as one is designated master and one is designated slave.
- Floppy cables
  - The controller connects into the floppy disk controller on the system board or into an add-in controller card.
  - There are four connectors at the other end, only two of which may be used at once.
- CD audio cable

  This is a cable that runs from the CD-ROM drive to an input on the sound card.

System Ports

- These are used to connect external devices to a PC.
- Serial ports
    - Bits of information are sent in a *series*, one at a time, in a straight line.
    - They are described as communications ports or COM ports and are numbered (COM 1, COM 2, etc.).
    - Serial ports support DB-9 or DB-25-pin connectors, with earlier PCs adopting the 25-pin standard and ATs the 9-pin.
    - Serial communication cables are no longer than 50 ft (15 m) in length.
- Parallel ports
    - Information is sent in *parallel*, 8 data bits at a time.
    - They are used to connect line printers and terminals together, also known as Line Print Terminals (LPTs).
    - Two parallel standards are Bi-Tronics (IEEE 1284) and Centronics.
    - Both specifications use a 25-pin D-shell (Centronics) connector.
- Universal Serial Bus (USB) ports

    Most modern computers will have at least two USB ports. They can be identified by their small rectangular shape.
- PS/2 ports

    These are sometimes color coded to make it easier to determine which port is for the keyboard and which is for the mouse.
- RJ-11

    This is a common telephone connector, typically found on modems.
- RJ-45

    These are connectors for Ethernet network cable, similar but larger than RJ-11.
- BNC

    This is a connector for cable wiring, commonly found on network cards.
- IEEE 1394 (FireWire)

    This is a rectangular box with six contacts.

Course Reference Material

Manual

- Chapter 5
- Chapter 13

Challenge! Interactive

- Installation, Configuration, and Upgrading

Exam Criteria

1.5 Identify proper procedures for installing and configuring IDE/EIDE devices.

Points to Remember

Installing

- Jumper the drive as either a master or a slave device.
- If installing a single IDE drive jumper, it is a master drive.
- If installing two drives on the same interface, one must be set as the master and the other as a slave.
- Mount the hard disk in the enclosure.
- Connect the power and drive cables.

  Make sure Pin 1 is oriented the correct direction, usually on the side facing the power cable.

Configuring

- Use the system's CMOS Setup program for configuring IDE disk drives.

- Newer Plug and Play BIOS can automatically detect and configure IDE hard drives when the drive type is set to Auto.

- If your drive type is not autodetected, then you must manually enter the parameters for the number of heads, cylinders, sectors per track, etc.

- It may be necessary to upgrade your BIOS to be able to properly recognize the hard drive.

Course Reference Material

Manual

- Chapter 7
  - o Installing a Disk Drive Adapter
  - o Hard Disk Installation

Challenge! Interactive

- Installation, Configuration, and Upgrading

Exam Criteria

1.6   Identify proper procedures for installing and configuring SCSI devices.

Points to Remember

Installation

- SCSI drives must be set to a unique ID that does not conflict with any other installed SCSI devices.

- If setting the hard drive as the boot drive, set the SCSI ID to zero.

- If the PC supports SCSI Plug and Play, you will not need to manually set jumpers to configure the drives's SCSI ID.

- The disk drive controller (or controller/data) cable must be terminated at the hard disk.

- If multiple drives are connected in a daisy-chained configuration, the last drive in the daisy-chain will be terminated.

- Mount the hard disk in the enclosure.

- Connect the power and drive cables.
- Multiple SCSI drives will be internally connected to a single daisy-chain cable.

Configuration

- In the CMOS, select No Drive Defined or equivalent setting.
- The disk controller translates disk information so that your physical hard disk logically emulates the selected configuration.
- Some disks may come bundled with a disk utility matched specifically to that drive or interface type.
- Select SCSI ID number.
- The SCSI bus must be terminated at each end of the chain.

Course Reference Material

Manual

- Chapter 7
  - o Hard Disk Installation

Challenge! Interactive

- Installation, Configuration, and Upgrading

Exam Criteria

1.7   Identify proper procedures for installing and configuring peripheral devices.

Points to Remember

Modem Installation

- Internal

  - Configure any jumpers on the modem card according to manufacturers directions and install the card into an available ISA or PCI slot.

  - If the card is Plug and Play, install software when requested by the operating system upon bootup.

  - The modem will take one of the four COM (serial) ports. Ensure that there is no conflict with an existing serial device.

- External

  - Simply connect the modem to an available serial or USB port on the system and connect a power adapter.

  - Usually no configuration is necessary.

Video Cards

- If necessary, jumper the card according to manufacturer specifications. Ensure that the appropriate IRQ and other addresses are available.

- Open the case and locate an ISA, PCI, or AGP open slot, depending on the type of adapter.

- Install the card into the slot.

- If Plug and Play is present, the system will automatically configure the system.

USB Peripherals

- The motherboard and operating system must support USB for the devices to work, and the CMOS USB option must be enabled.

- Supporting operating systems include Windows 95 OSR2 and newer.

- It may be necessary to upgrade or flash the BIOS to properly recognize the adapter.

- Install the card into an open slot on the motherboard.

- Plug and Play will automatically detect and configure the card. The combination of all USB devices will need only one IRQ.

IEEE 1284 (Parallel Port)

- All modern computers come with one parallel port that is enabled in the BIOS.

- A second may be installed in any open ISA or PCI slot.

- Configure any jumpers and install the card into the slot.

- Enable support for a second LPT port in the BIOS.

- If Plug and Play is present, the card will automatically be configured.

IEEE 1394 (FireWire)

- Locate an open ISA or PCI slot on the motherboard; most IEEE 1394 adapters will be PCI.

- Install the adapter in the slot.

- All current FireWire adapters are Plug and Play and will be configured by the operating system. Windows 98 supports IEEE 1394.

Portable Peripheral Device Installation

- Docking stations and port replicators are devices that extend the capabilities and ease of connecting external devices to laptops.

  No physical installation is necessary; simply load the software provided by the manufacturer.

- PC Cards need only be slid into the appropriate type1, type2, or type3 slot while the power is off. They will be recognized by Plug and Play when booted. Install drivers and software as directed by the manufacturer when recognized by the operating system.

Course Reference Material

Manual

- Chapter 3
- Chapter 7

Digital Video

- Touring the Inside of a PC
- Installing Components

Challenge! Interactive

- Installation, Configuration, and Upgrading

Exam Criteria

1.8 Identify hardware methods of upgrading system performance, procedures for replacing basic subsystem components, and unique components and when to use them.

Points to Remember

Memory

- Increasing memory is the easiest and most cost-effective way to increase the speed of a computer.

- Additional memory may be required by an operating system upgrade or new applications.

- Consult the motherboard's manufacturer for the maximum amount of memory the board will support.

- Open the case and locate memory slots.

  If there are no empty slots, but the computer has additional memory capacity, it may be necessary to remove existing memory sticks to replace with larger-capacity modules.

- Simply install the memory modules in the slots and reboot the system. They should be automatically detected by the system.

Hard Drives

- Faster hard drives with additional capacity can increase performance and storage capacity in computers.

- A new drive may be installed in place of the existing drive or added to the existing drive as slave on the same IDE cable or on a separate cable.

- It may be necessary to upgrade the BIOS in order to recognize a larger drive or run a manufacturer's software to enable proper recognition of the new drive by the BIOS.

CPU

- A cost-effective way to increase speed and processing power is to upgrade the CPU.

- Motherboards support a number of different CPU speeds of the same type of processor. It is frequently possible to install a faster processor without installing a new motherboard.

- Jumpers will usually have to be reset on the motherboard to manufacturer's specifications for voltage, clock speed, etc.

Upgrading the BIOS

- Upgrading the system BIOS may be necessary or desirable to fix motherboard support bugs, increase hard drive or peripheral capacity, provide support for new technologies, or support a new operating system or other software.

- The BIOS can usually be upgraded by downloading a file from the manufacturer's Web site, creating a boot disk with the file, and booting to the disk to install the BIOS.

- If the BIOS cannot be upgraded, it may be replaceable, in which case, it may be removed with a chip puller and a new one installed.

Course Reference Material

Manual

- Chapter 7
  - Installing a Disk Drive Adapter
  - Hard Disk Installation

Challenge! Interactive

- Installation, Configuration, and Upgrading

DOMAIN 2.0 DIAGNOSING AND TROUBLESHOOTING

Exam Criteria

2.1   Identify common symptoms and problems associated with each module and how to troubleshoot and isolate the problems.

Points to Remember

System Boards

- If POST error codes are present, refer to the manufacturer's BIOS code list.
- If a system is not booting, check for signs that the system is getting power.
- Check the power supply with a multimeter.
- Remove all expansion cards from the system and reseat.
- Use a diagnostic card that plugs into the expansion bus.

Disk Drives

Check data cable, drive jumpers, and power cable.

CD-ROM

- If the CD-ROM drive is not recognized, reseat the cable connectors.
- Check the system BIOS to make sure the IDE interface is enabled.
- Check to see if you can access a CD-ROM from the DOS command prompt.
- Try several different CD-ROMs in the drive.

Tape Drives

- Use proper tapes.
- Clean the read/write head and entire tape path after every 25 hours of use.

Controllers and Adapters

- Try cleaning the edge contacts and then reseat the adapter.
- If the card is installed correctly, you may have an IRQ or DMA conflict.

Monitors

- No power
  - Make sure the monitor is plugged in and power is applied.
  - Unplug the power cord from the monitor and check the voltage.
  - If voltage is present at the power cord and if no LEDs are lit, check the fuse.
- No display
  - Reseat the video cable.
  - Swap the video cable with one that is known to work.
  - Swap the monitor with one that is working. If the new monitor does not work, reseat or replace the video board inside the PC. If the new monitor *does* work, the problem resides inside the original monitor.
  - Listen for the distant crackling sound of high voltage; if this sound is not present, it may indicate a faulty high-voltage power supply.
- Missing colors
  - Reseat the video cable and video card and check for damaged/missing pins.
  - Swap out cable and monitor.
- Distorted display
  Check for EMI.

Modems

- Check cables, wall jack, and power.
- Complete analog loopback test.
- Complete analog loopback self-test.
- Complete remote digital loopback as needed.
- Software issues
  - Check connect rate in software.
  - Check for line noise.
  - If external modem, check for source of EMI.
  - Check flow control settings on your computer and the modem.
  - Echo on/off can cause you to not see messages on the screen or to see double characters for everything you type.

Ports

To test an RS-232 port, you will need a breakout box with indicator lights and a diagnostics program such as Pdiags.exe.

Cable

To test the cable, attach one end of it to the port and the other end to the breakout box.

Keyboards

- Vacuum keyboards on a regular basis to avoid accumulation of foreign matter.
- If there is a spill, flush out the keyboard with clean water, then let it dry completely, at least 24 hours, before testing.
- Check DIN connector on PC with voltmeter.

PS/2-Style Keyboard Connector

- Use a multimeter to check the continuity in the cable.
- Check a keyboard problem with a known good keyboard.

Mouse

Check connections, remove mouse ball, and clean rollers.

Touch pads

Check driver, connection, and IRQ/address problems.

Microphones

- Check connections, battery, and drivers.
- Check on another sound card.

Scanners

- If a parallel scanner, check for conflicts with another parallel port device.
- Check drivers and run manufacturer's diagnostics.
- Check the parallel port and cable connections.

Course Reference Material

Manual

- Chapter 8

Challenge! Interactive

- Diagnosing and Troubleshooting

Exam Criteria

2.2 Identify basic troubleshooting procedures and how to elicit problem symptoms from customers.

Points to Remember

Troubleshooting Communication Skills

- Effective listening techniques
    - Face-to-face techniques

        Greet customer, maintain eye contact, exercise positive body language, practice thorough note taking.
    - Telephone techniques
        - Practice active listening.
        - Remain calm and use rules of telephone etiquette.
        - Give your customer a verbal confirmation of the problem in the conversation and then repeat the problem.
- Questioning skills
    - Open-ended questioning techniques

        When asked, these give your customer the unlimited freedom to answer as he/she wishes.
    - Close-ended questioning techniques
        - Pose your question as more of a statement, then ask for a yes or no confirmation.
        - When dealing with difficult situations, use ALERT: Acknowledge, Listen, Empathize, Respond, Thank.

- Setting expectations
  - o Establish a working partnership with your customer.
  - o Promise only what you can deliver.
  - o Set realistic resolution time frames.
  - o Document commitments and dates.
  - o Never offer an unrealistic solution to your customer.
- Following up
  - o Deliver on commitments, time frames, and solutions.
  - o Solicit suggestions for service and process improvements.

Wave's DIReCtional Troubleshooting Model

- Define the problem.
  - o Description
  - o Type
  - o Conditions present
- Isolate the occurrence.
  - o Classify as hardware or software.
  - o Re-create the problem.
  - o Document all results.
- Resolve the problem.
  - o Use technical documentation, your notes, and the Internet to research the problem.
  - o Identify likely causes.
  - o Solve the problem and repeat your solution.
  - o Document the steps that you took to resolve the malfunction.
- Confirm the resolution and expectations.
  - o Review the case history of the problem to ensure that no steps were missed.
  - o Is the user happy with the solution?

Course Reference Material

Manual

- Chapter 6

Challenge! Interactive

- Diagnosing and Troubleshooting

DOMAIN 3.0 SAFETY AND PREVENTIVE MAINTENANCE

Exam Criteria

3.1 Identify the purpose of various types of preventive maintenance products and procedures and when to use and perform them.

Points to Remember

Preventive Maintenance

- Tools
  - A clean, damp cloth
  - Canned (compressed) air or a vacuum cleaner
  - A small brush or cotton swab
  - Glass cleaner
  - A lint-free cloth
  - CD-ROM and floppy drive cleaning kits
  - OS maintenance software
- Cleaning with a damp cloth
  - Outside of case
  - Inside of cover
  - Monitor screen with antiglare

- Canned air and small brush
  - System board
  - Expansion cards
  - CPU fan
  - Keyboard
  - Mouse ball and rollers (cotton swab)
- Vacuum and small brush

Power supply fan

- Glass cleaner and lint-free cloth

Monitor with antiglare

- Commercial cleaning kits

These should be used to clean heads, spindles, etc., on floppy drives and CD-ROMs.

- Lint-free cloth

CD disks (wipe from middle to outside)

- Reinstall any expansion cards that have been removed from the computer and check and reseat any loose socket chips.
- OS maintenance software

Defragment the hard drive and perform a surface scan that checks for bad sectors.

Course Reference Material

Manual

- Chapter 6
  - Ongoing Maintenance

Challenge! Interactive

- Safety and Preventive Maintenance

Exam Criteria

3.2   Identify issues, procedures, and devices for protection within the computing environment, including people, hardware, and the surrounding workspace.

Points to Remember

Safety Tips to Protect the Technician

- Never work alone.
- Always use protective eyewear or safety goggles.
- Always wear shoes with nonconductive rubber soles.
- Never assume that an electrical device is safe to handle.
- Perform your tests with the device disconnected from the power source.
- Always disconnect the power from a device when you are connecting or removing test leads.
- Current over 0.03 amps is potentially fatal and generally more dangerous than high voltage.
- Do not wear jewelry of any kind.
- Always discharge the large capacitors in equipment power supplies if you intend to remove the protective housing.

Potential Hazards with Computer Equipment

- Electrical outlets
  - Three prongs as follows:
    - Large slot is neutral, black wire.
    - Small slot is hot (phase), white wire.
    - Hole is ground, green wire.
  - Check using Volt-Ohm-Milliammeter (VOM) meter set to read in the 120-VAC range.
- Power supply
  - There are no user-serviceable parts inside a power supply.
  - If you must work on a power supply, you should first discharge the capacitor.

- Monitors

  o The CRT is vacuum sealed and, if broken, will implode, throwing shards of glass in every direction.

  o If you will be working on the interior of a monitor, it is important that you discharge the CRT to prevent a *lethal* electric discharge.

- Printers

  o Before repairing a printer, always disconnect the printer from the power source.

  o The print head on dot-matrix printers and the fuser assembly in laser printers can cause burns.

  o Light generated by laser printers is not visible to the eye but can damage your eyes.

- Fire extinguishers and computers

  The best Class C fire extinguisher for use in a computer-related fire is a Class BC Halon or CO_2 extinguisher.

- Working environment and storage

  Power protection

  o Surge protectors

    - Protect your system and peripherals from any over-voltage conditions.

    - These are rated by *clamping voltage* and *clamping speed*.

  o Standby power supplies

    - These are constantly charged from the AC outlet, and in case of a power failure, the computer is switched over to the battery.

    - There is usually no surge protection.

  o Uninterruptible Power Supply (UPS)

    - The computer is connected directly to the battery, which is connected to the outlet, so there is no switching.

    - It also insulates the computer from spikes, surges, and other inconsistencies of electricity.

- Electrostatic Discharge (ESD)
  - Transistor-Transistor Logic (TTL) chips are more robust than the newer Complementary Metal Oxide Semiconductor (CMOS) chips and not as susceptible.
  - Prevention
    - Keep relative humidity of 50% or higher.
    - Connect the equipment and an antistatic wrist strap to a common ground to keep all electron levels in balance.
    - Use commercial wrist straps manufactured with a resistor on it.
    - Keep all electronic components in their protective antistatic bags (Faraday cages) and foam until you are ready to connect them.
  - ESD workstation
    - Use a conductive rubber mat on a suitable work surface.
    - Place the computer on the rubber mat.
    - Connect the wire (supplied with the mat) to the bare metal frame of the computer chassis.
    - Connect the wrist strap to the computer chassis.
  - ESD vs. Electromagnetic Interference (EMI)
    - Electrostatic Discharge (ESD) is a static discharge issue that can destroy components.
    - Electromagnetic Interference (EMI) is a magnetic field (caused when electromagnetic energy is leaked into free space) that interacts with other electronic circuits or magnetic fields.
- Disposal of equipment
  - Rather than disposal, the best option for proper management of *retired* computer equipment is recycling all useable parts.
  - Federal law prohibits corporations from dumping CRTs (monitors) in landfills.
  - Many batteries, including all batteries used by portable computers, contain hazardous materials that must be recycled.
  - Toner and ink cartridges should also be recycled.

Course Reference Material

Manual

- Chapter 2

Challenge! Interactive

- Safety and Preventive Maintenance

DOMAIN 4.0 MOTHERBOARD/PROCESSORS/MEMORY

Exam Criteria

4.1   Distinguish between the popular CPU chips in terms of their basic characteristics.

Points to Remember

Microprocessors

- The microprocessor is the nucleus of the computer.
- Performance variables are as follows:

CPU speed	Number of cycles per second in MHz or GHz
Microcode	Binary instruction executed by the CPU
Word size	The largest number handled in one operation in bits
Data path	The largest size of input and output during one cycle in bits
Memory	The maximum amount of memory the chip can address in MB or GB

- Intel processors

8080	Still found in many specialized, low-level applications, such as household appliances
8088	4.77 MHz to 8 MHz, 40-pin DIP
8086	Essentially the same as 8088 but lower pin count
80286	16-bit data path, Pin Grid Array
80386SX	16-bit data path, Memory Management Unit, up to 4 GB of memory

80386DX	32-bit data path
80486DX	32-bit data path, 386 chip, 385 cache controller chip (8 KB), 387 math coprocessor chip; up to 4 GB of memory
80486SX	Same as DX except math coprocessor is disabled
Pentium	64-bit internal and external bus, 60 MHz to 200 MHz, up to four instructions per clock cycle, two 8-KB caches, up to 4 GB of memory; full support for multitasking environments; Socket 4 is 60 to 66 MHz, Socket 5 is 75 to 133 MHz, Socket 7 is 105 to 200 MHz
Pentium MMX	32-KB cache, 57 new instructions to speed the processing of multimedia content
Pentium Pro	New architecture including Dynamic Execution, 64 bits, 150 to 200 MHz, scalable to four microprocessors, 4 GB of memory, 387-pin Dual-Independent Bus (DIB)
Pentium II	233 to 450 MHz, MMX technology is included; 66-MHz bus went to 100-MHz bus with the 350-MHz processor; uses a Slot 1 Single Edge Contact Cartridge (SECC); 512 KB of L2 cache
Pentium II Xeon	Same as Pentium II but with 512-KB, 1-MB, or 2-MB L2 cache; for servers running 8 or more processors, Slot 2
Celeron	Original version was simply a Pentium II processor with no L2 cache and a 66-MHz system bus, starting with 300 MHz; included a 128-KB cache running at the same speed as the processor
Pentium III	70 new multimedia instructions called Internet Streaming SIMD Extensions (SSE), 450 MHz to 1+ GHz, 133-MHz system bus, L2 cache running at the same clock speed as the processor, Slot 1
Pentium 4	Entirely new processor core, support for a 400-MHz system bus and SSE2, which adds 144 new instructions; processor speed of 1.4 GHz
AMD-K6/K6-2 MMX	64-KB L1 cache; the K6 is 166 to 233 MHz; the K6-2 is up to 550 MHz, Socket 7

3DNow!	3DNow! Technology; set of 21 instructions that use SIMD and other performance enhancements to improve 3-D graphics performance
AMD Athlon	Adds 24 instructions to the 21 original 3DNow! instructions, Slot A Single Edge Contact (SEC), newer-use Socket A, 200- to 266-MHz system bus, faster FPU than K6 line
AMD Duron	Based on the AMD Athlon core but uses a smaller L2 cache, 200-MHz system bus
Cyrix6x86MX/MX-II chips	Marked with a speed rating, MMX instructions incorporated, use existing Pentium motherboards, 64 KB of write-back cache
Cyrix MIII	Socket 370-based system boards, poor FPU performance, and low clock speeds

Course Reference Material

Manual

- Chapter 3
    - o   Microprocessors

Digital Video

- Touring the Inside of a PC
- Installing Components

Challenge! Interactive

- Motherboard/Processors/Memory

Exam Criteria

4.2   Identify the categories of RAM (Random Access Memory) terminology, their locations, and physical characteristics.

Points to Remember

System Memory

- Parity and nonparity memory

  Parity memory adds an extra bit for every 8 bits of data (total 9) and is used for error detection, but it is not widely implemented.

- Random Access Memory (RAM) is volatile storage, meaning that the information is lost if the system is powered down or restarted.

  o   Dynamic RAM (DRAM) chips must have electrical current supplied to maintain their electrical state, read in nanoseconds (ns).

  o   Fast Page Mode (FPM) has improved memory controller.

  o   With Extended Data Output (EDO), the CPU can access memory 10% to 15% faster than similar FPM DRAM chips.

  o   Synchronous DRAM (SDRAM) is synchronized to the system clock.

  o   Double Data Rate (DDR) SDRAM uses data strobe.

  o   Rambus DRAM (RDRAM) allows data transfer through a very simple bus operating at high speeds.

  o   Static RAM (SRAM) chips do not need electrical current for refresh purposes; SRAM is much faster than DRAM and is most commonly used as cache memory.

- Memory packaging

  o   Single In-Line Memory Module (SIMM) is available in 1 MB to 64 MB, is used with AT-compatible systems, and has two types, 30- and 72-pin, installed in pairs of identical chips.

  o   Dual In-Line Memory Module (DIMM) is 168 pin and 64 bits wide. PC100 and PC133 are the industry standards; most use SDRAM.

  o   Rambus In-Line Memory Module (RIMM)–PC600, PC700, and PC800–has a theoretical peak data transfer rate of 1.6 GB per second.

  o   Video RAM (VRAM) is designed specifically for video adapters and prevents flickering.

- o   Window RAM (WRAM) is used on graphic-intensive systems, achieves faster performance at less cost than VRAM because it supports addressing of large blocks (*windows*) of video memory, and uses dual data ports.

- o   Synchronous Graphics RAM (SGRAM) is an enhancement of SDRAM for graphic-specific features; it retrieves and modifies data in blocks.

- o   Flash RAM is nonvolatile memory, can be upgraded with software, and is used primarily for mobile computers.

- •   Laptop memory

- o   This is frequently proprietary in design.

- o   Many laptops now are able to use Small Outline Dual In-Line Memory Modules (SODIMMs), which are functionally similar to standard SIMMs and DIMMs but are smaller, about one third as thick, and come in 72- and 144-pin versions.

Course Reference Material

Manual

- •   Chapter 3

- o   System Memory

- o   Laptop Components

Digital Video

- •   Touring the Inside of a PC

- •   Installing Components

Challenge! Interactive

- •   Motherboard/Processors/Memory

Exam Criteria

4.3   Identify the most popular type of motherboards, their components, and their architecture (bus structures and power supplies).

Points to Remember

System Boards (Motherboard)

- Components include processor, chipset circuitry, RAM slots, system bus (external bus), mouse, keyboard, USB, serial, and parallel port connectors.
- System board performance issues are based on processor speed, configuration, memory, buses, chipset circuitry, and software support.
- ATX motherboard

  Advantages over AT include provides 90-degree rotation of slots, more space for expansion cards, fewer cables, better ventilation and cooling, and lower cost.

- Support circuitry
  - External bus

    This connects the microprocessor to the supporting circuitry of the computer.
  - Address bus

    When the microprocessor wants to communicate with another device, it selects that device using the address bus and an address specific to that device.
  - Data bus

    It is the path the data takes from the microprocessor to a device located on the external bus.

- Firmware
  - System BIOS
    - This contains all of the software required to control all other basic functions of the system board and can be periodically updated with new software to fix bugs and add support for new technologies.
    - If the BIOS is stored on a ROM BIOS chip, the entire chip must be replaced whenever the software needs to be updated.

o   System CMOS

- PC hardware configuration information is stored in CMOS RAM and is maintained by a battery.

- CMOS settings can be adjusted in the BIOS Setup.

• Laptop components

o   Laptop memory is frequently proprietary in design, and most are able to use Small Outline Dual In-Line Memory Modules (SODIMMs).

o   Batteries

- Nickel-Cadmium (NiCad) batteries have a life span of around 1,000 cycles, are toxic to the environment, and suffer from memory effect.

- Nickel Metal-Hydride (NiMH) batteries provide about twice the electrical storage capacity of NiCad batteries and suffer less from the memory effect than NiCad batteries.

- Lithium-Ion (Li-Ion) batteries provide approximately 35% more power than NiMH batteries, do not suffer from the memory effect, and are more environmentally friendly than NiCad or NiMH batteries because they do not contain toxic materials such as Cadmium or Mercury.

o   Flash RAM hard disks are very fast, are typically housed in type II PCMCIA cards, and are made of Flash Memory chips.

o   Personal Computer Memory Card Industry Association (PCMCIA) was introduced in 1990 as a bus designed for miniaturization or for use in notebook and subnotebook computers. The name was later changed to PC Card and now uses CardBus technology, which is similar to PCI and allows the cards to run at 33 MHz with a 32-bit bus.

- Type I is 3.3 mm thick. These slots work only with memory expansion cards.

- Type II accepts cards 5 mm thick and type I cards, and supports modems, SCSI, sound cards, network adapters, etc.

- Type III is 10.5 mm thick and is intended primarily for computers with removable hard drives.

- Expansion buses
  - The expansion bus is a set of circuitry, traces, and conducting lines that run in parallel across the system board and connect the microprocessor to the expansion slots on the system board.

  - Terminology
    - Bandwidth is a measurement of how much data the bus can carry.

    - Bus mastering is a process whereby devices can take control of the system bus.

    - Bus speed reflects how many bits of information can be sent across each wire each second.

  - ISA bus (AT bus)
    - It supports 16-bit slots and uses both sides of the card for connections. The microprocessor acts like a traffic cop coordinating all activity across the bus, including data transfers, modem communications, and graphics control.

    - Requests have to go through the DMA controller and are not tailored to peripheral devices doing large block transfers.

  - Micro Channel Architecture (MCA)
    - This is used mostly in IBM PS/2 systems.

    - It is a bus-driven architecture that allows intelligent devices to request and gain access to the bus (bus mastering) to communicate directly with memory.

    - It comes in both 16-bit and 32-bit versions and supports 16 MB of memory.

  - EISA
    - The EISA bus was built on the older ISA standard by adding more address lines, more data lines, and more control signals.

    - Like MCA, intelligent devices are allowed to take control of the system bus and perform large data transfers directly to memory.

    - EISA can reach a peak transfer rate of 33 MBps and is 50% faster than IBM's original implementation of MCA.

  - Local buses

    These provide an I/O channel for a device, e.g., a video card, directly to the processor using a 32- or 64-bit path, the speed of which is determined by the external speed of the processor.

- o   VESA Local Bus (VL-Bus)

  - The original version utilized a 32-bit data path with a maximum 40-MHz bus speed. A throughput of VL-Bus is 133 MBps (at 33 MHz) compared to 8 MBps for the ISA bus.

  - The most important feature of the VL-Bus is its ability to standardize a connector and protocol for bus expansion.

- o   Peripheral Component Interconnect (PCI)

  - PCI uses a 32- or 64-bit path for data transfer with a maximum throughput in 32-bit operation of 132 MBps and in 64-bit of 264 MBps.

  - It is processor independent and supports the Plug and Play standard implemented with Windows 95.

- o   Accelerated Graphics Port (AGP)

  - This was designed specifically for the throughput requirements of 3-D graphics.

  - AGP 1x is based on the PCI specification, is 32 bits wide, runs at 66 MHz, and could transfer data at a rate of up to 266 MBps.

    It is now available to support AGP 2x and AGP 4x, which can transfer data at rates of 533 MBps and 1.07 GBps, respectively.

- o   Plug and Play (PnP) eliminates the need of manually configuring the system and moving hardware jumpers when adding new peripherals.

  It is supported directly in Windows 95, 98, and 2000 on systems with system BIOS PnP support.

- o   Universal Serial Bus (USB)

  - Resources are dynamically allocated as needed to up to 127 devices at once with power, as well as data, carried on the USB cable.

  - To be compatible with USB, the host controller must use the Open Host Controller Interface (OpenHCI) and the Universal Host Controller Interface (UHCI) standards.

  - It is partially supported in Windows 95 OSR2 and fully supported in Windows 98 and 2000.

  - There are two transfer rates:

    - o   1.5 Mbps is used by low-bandwidth devices.

    - o   12 Mbps is used by high-bandwidth devices.

  - Topology is made up of host, hub, and device.

- o IEEE 1394 FireWire

    - This was developed for high-bandwidth devices such as digital cameras, digital camcorders, and video disc players.

    - It allows the direct connection of up to 63 devices, supports up to 256 TB of memory, and is Plug and Play compatible.

    - Topology is made up of device, splitter, bridge, and repeater.

    - Bus transfer rates are from 98 Mbps to 393 Mbps.

  - o Infrared devices

      These allow a computer to transfer data from one device to another without any cables.

- Power supplies

  - o 4 outputs: +12 volts, -12 volts, +5 volts, and -5 volts

  - o AT: Two 6-pin black-to-black Burndy connectors (P8 and P9)

  - o ATX: 20-pin connector called a Molex connector and routes the on/off switch through the system board

Course Reference Material

Manual

- Chapter 3

  - o System Boards

  - o Expansion Bus

- Chapter 5

- Chapter 7

  - o System Board Configuration

Digital Video

- Touring the Inside of a PC

- Installing Components

Challenge! Interactive

- Motherboard/Processors/Memory

Exam Criteria

4.4   Identify the purpose of CMOS (Complementary Metal Oxide Semiconductor), what it contains, and how to change its basic parameters.

Points to Remember

CMOS

- The method for entering CMOS varies from manufacturer to manufacturer but is frequently the *DELETE* key, *F1*, or *F2*.

- The user is presented with a menu upon entering.

- Common device settings
  - o   Standard Setup

    Date & Time, floppy configuration, hard drive configuration
  - o   BIOS Features

    Boot order, system cache, system memory
  - o   Chipset Features

    Memory timing, system board configuration
  - o   Power Management

    Power management features, hard drive power-saving modes
  - o   Enable/Edit Password
  - o   PNP/PCI Configuration

    Modify the Plug and Play behavior.
  - o   Load BIOS Defaults
  - o   Load Setup Defaults

    Sets the BIOS to the most conservative settings possible
  - o   IDE HDD Auto Detection
  - o   Save & Exit Setup
  - o   Exit Without Saving

- BIOS replacement/updating
  - ○ Support additional types or large-capacity disk drives
  - ○ Provide compatibility with applications or new operating systems and environments
  - ○ Procedure to replace

    Remove the old BIOS chips with a chip puller and insert the new BIOS chips.
  - ○ Procedure to upgrade

    Download the correct BIOS for your system and flash according to the directions provided.

Course Reference Material

Manual

- Chapter 7
  - ○ CMOS

Challenge! Interactive

- Motherboard/Processors/Memory

DOMAIN 5.0 PRINTERS

Exam Criteria

5.1   Identify basic concepts, printer operations, and printer components.

Points to Remember

Types of Printers

- Dot-matrix printers
    - These are for printing on multipart (carbon copy) tractor-feed forms.
    - They employ a series of pins, also called print wires, that strike a ribbon placed between the paper and the print head.
    - They commonly use 9, 18, or 24 pins.
    - Operation
        - The print head contains a large permanent magnet that pulls the spring-loaded print wires toward it.
        - An electromagnet coil is wrapped around the print wire, and when power is applied to the coil, the print wire is repelled from the permanent magnet.
        - When the print wire makes contact with the print ribbon and stops, the permanent magnet overcomes the force of the spring and starts the print wire moving in the opposite direction.
    - They support both high-quality or Near Letter Quality (NLQ) and lower-quality (draft quality) print modes.
- Ink-jet printers
    - An ink-jet printer sprays droplets of ink directly on the paper.
    - Some ink-jets use a piezo-electric crystal that squeezes the ink out by subjecting it to an electrical current.
    - Some ink-jets use a small heating element that boils the ink, developing steam that forces the ink out of the nozzle.
    - They typically use either a parallel or USB interface.
    - Paper is fed through a series of powered rollers with speed measured in pages per minute (ppm).

- Laser printers
  - These use a laser beam to form a high-resolution image ranging from 300 dpi to more than 1,200 dpi.
  - The two popular control languages that are used with laser printers are PostScript and PCL.
  - They may be serial, parallel, or USB.
  - The six-step electro-photostatic (EP) process is as follows:
    - Cleaning

      This scrapes any residual toner from the drum.
    - Conditioning

      The corona wire applies a uniform negative charge on the drum.
    - Writing

      A laser beam strikes the surface of the drum, placing dots and forming a latent image with a neutral electrical charge.
    - Developing

      The developer roller (or toner cylinder) attracts negatively charged toner particles that are rolled onto, and adhere to, the latent image areas of the drum.
    - Transferring

      The transfer roller or transfer corona transfers a positive charge to the paper and attracts the image with toner.
    - Fusing

      The fuser roller heats the toner sufficiently to cause it to melt, then the pressure roller presses the melted toner into the paper.

Course Reference Material

Manual

- Chapter 9

Challenge! Interactive

- Printers

Exam Criteria

5.2   Identify care and service techniques and common problems with primary printer types.

Points to Remember

Potential Hazards from Printers

- Always disconnect the power source unless absolutely necessary during servicing.
- The print head on dot-matrix printers and the fuser assembly in laser printers must be allowed to cool after operation before servicing.
- The light generated by laser printers is not visible but can damage your eyes.

Potential Hazards to Printers

- Surge protectors can be used to protect printers from any over-voltage conditions.
- Use ESD protection when handling logic boards or other printer electronics.

Basic Printer Troubleshooting

- Not printing
  - o   Check power.
  - o   Check paper.
  - o   Check driver and settings.
- Printing garbage
  - o   Check connections and cable.
  - o   Clear all pending documents, then reinitialize the printer. Try printing a different document.

- Network printer is not responding.
  - Verify that the connections are solid.
  - Verify that the user is logged on to the network and has security rights to access.
  - Verify that the print job is being sent to the correct print queue.
  - Verify that the printer is online.
- Dot-matrix print appears too light.
  - Check the print head spacing.
  - Check the ribbon.
  - Check the paper transport mechanism.
- Dot-matrix printer is not responding properly to line feeds and form feeds.
  - Check the paper transport mechanism.
  - Check the correct print driver.
- Black or white bands of ink appear throughout the document when using an ink-jet printer.
  - This is often caused by a clogged nozzle.
  - Check for a defective ribbon cable.
  - Check the print head.
- The laser printer is having problems with misfeeds and paper jams.
  - Check paper for proper basis weight and caliper.
  - If several pages pulled through the printer at once try a heavier paper.
  - If heavy paper must be used, use the paper path with the fewest number of bends.
  - When opening a ream, *break* the ream rather than fan the sheets.
- Background images and splattered toner

  Try a rougher paper.
- Stripes across the laser printer documents
  - Toner may be low.
  - If vertical stripes, you may have a damaged drum unit.
  - Try switching to a smoother paper.

Course Reference Material

Manual

- Chapter 2
    - o   Potential Hazards with Computer Equipment
    - o   Potential Hazards to Computer Equipment
- Chapter 10

Challenge! Interactive

- Printers

DOMAIN 6.0 BASIC NETWORKING

Exam Criteria

6.1   Identify basic networking concepts, including how a network works and the ramifications of repairs on the network.

Points to Remember

Local Area Network (LAN)

- A LAN is a group of computers running a specialized communications software and joined through an external data path.
    - o   Small geographic area (single building)
    - o   Direct high-speed connection between all workstations and servers
    - o   Shared hardware resources and data files
    - o   Centralized management of resources and network security
    - o   Each server and workstation will have at least one network adapter, often called a Network Interface Card (NIC).
    - o   The cable plant is the communications path between the server(s) and workstations.

- Client/Server
  - o Separate systems provide resources (servers) and access resources (clients).
  - o Resource and security management is fully centralized.
  - o The Network Operating System (NOS) runs at the server.
- Peer-to-peer (workgroup)
  - o Systems both provide and receive services with no centralized server.
  - o Resource and security management is handled at the individual system level.

Wide Area Network (WAN)

- WANs are expanded LANs.
  - o Wide geographic area
  - o Low- to high-speed links
  - o Remote links
  - o In most cases, WANs support data transmissions across public carriers.

Campus Area Network (CAN)

These are connected networks in geographically contiguous buildings.

Metropolitan Area Network (MAN)

These connect networks that are noncontiguous but located within a local calling area.

The OSI Model

- This was developed by the International Organization for Standardization (ISO) during the late 1970s.
- The seven layers
    - Physical layer

        This layer defines the mechanical and electrical characteristics of the cables and connectors that link the network components.
    - Data Link layer

        - This specifies how devices attached to the network gain access to the various computing resources.

        - These are two sublayers.

            - Logical Link Control (LLC)

            - Media Access Control (MAC)
    - Network layer

        This layer is responsible for establishing a unique network address and managing the transport of information packets between different networks.
    - Transport layer

        - This is responsible for the accuracy of the data transmission; it maintains overall management and control responsibilities.

        - The Network layer combined with the Transport layer define the full functionality of network operating systems.
    - Session layer

        This layer is responsible for the integrity of the logical connection of the software session.
    - Presentation layer

        This translates data into an appropriate transmission format.
    - Application layer

        This layer provides a series of definitions that are used to provide networkwide system management functions.

Network Topologies

- Bus topology
    - This is a linear transmission medium that is terminated at both ends.
    - Any break in the bus causes the entire network to become inoperable.
    - The bus topology is frequently implemented in a star configuration.
    - This is usually Ethernet.
- Ring topology
    - This is a closed-loop configuration.
    - Any break in the bus causes the entire network to become inoperable.
    - Most rings are actually wired in a star topology to isolate faults.
    - FDDI data-link protocol adds fault tolerance to the basic ring topology with a dual fiber-optic ring configuration that provides complete redundancy.
- Star topology
    - This connects the peripheral devices via point-to-point links to a central hub.
    - There is greater fault tolerance since a problem with one cable connection will not affect the other workstation nodes.
- Mesh topology
    - Each device has a point-to-point connection to every other device on the network.
    - There is a very high level of fault tolerance since if there is a network break, several alternate routes are available.
    - There is high complexity and cost.
- Cellular topology
    - This breaks a designated area into *cells*, each with a hub that services the cell's area.
    - The hubs are interconnected in order to provide end-to-end communications within the entire network.
    - Devices are allowed to physically relocate while maintaining a connection to the network.

Data-Link Protocols

- Protocols function at the second layer of the Open Systems Interconnection (OSI) model.
- Ethernet (IEEE 802.3)
  - This uses the Carrier Sense Multiple Access/Collision Detection (CSMA/CD) access method.
    - Carrier Sense—All nodes listen to the network for data transport.
    - Multiple Access—All nodes have concurrent access to the media.
    - Collision Detection—If two or more systems transmit at once, a *collision* occurs. The Network Interface Card (NIC) realizes the message did not get through and repeats the message.

    If a collision is detected, each station will wait for a randomly determined interval before retransmitting.
  - Thin Ethernet 10Base2 (Thinnet)
    - Linear bus topology
    - Uses British Naval Connector (BNC) T-connectors that attach workstations to the cable and terminators at either end
    - Uses a 0.2-in., 50-ohm cable
  - Thick Ethernet 10Base5
    - Linear bus topology
    - Uses a 0.4-in., 50-ohm coaxial cable
    - Uses BNC T-connectors that attach workstations to the cable and terminators at either end
  - Twisted-Pair 10BaseT
    - Most common choice
    - Star topology
    - Hubs may be linked together with number of stations set by total number of hub ports.
    - RJ-45 connectors are used to connect devices.

- Token Ring and 802.5
    - Logical ring is usually wired as a physical star.
    - It uses UTP, STP, or fiber optic.
    - Token (data frame) passes between systems, and any system can attach data to a token if the token is free (empty).
    - When a station detects a hard error, it begins to transmit beacon frames, which are used to define a failure domain.
    - Token Ring networks look like a star, but they work as a ring using Multistation Access Units (MSAUs).

Cabling

- Twisted Pair (TP)
    - Unshielded Twisted Pair (UTP)
        - UTP is a set of twisted pairs within a plastic sheath.
        - Category 3 cable supports data transport rates up to 10 Mbps.
        - Category 5 cable supports data transport rates up to 100 Mbps.
    - Shielded Twisted Pair (STP)

    It includes a protective sheathing around the copper wire.

- Coaxial cable
    - This is composed of two conductors that share the same axis. The center cable is insulated by plastic foam, a second conductor, foil wrap, and an external plastic tube.
    - It may be either baseband or broadband.

Ethernet Cable Connectors

- BNC is considered a 2-pin connector; Pin 1 is the inner wire, and Pin 2 is the tinned copper braid.
- An AUI connector is used for connecting to Thicknet transceivers.
- The RJ-45 connector is an 8-pin modular plug. Pins 1, 2, 3, and 6 are required to transport data according to the 10BaseT specification.
- Token Ring cable has a DB-9 connector at one end and an IBM-style hermaphroditic data connector at the other.

Fiber Distributed Data Interface (FDDI)

- FDDI supports LAN traffic at speeds of up to 100 Mbps.

- It is well suited to support security and video-intensive multimedia applications because of its fiber-optic infrastructure.

- Fault tolerance is provided by the dual-counter rotating ring architecture.

  In the event of a fiber break, the *wrap* feature will bypass the break by transferring data from the primary to the secondary ring.

Fiber-Optic Cable

- This is comprised of light-conducting glass encased in plastic fibers surrounded by a protective cladding and a durable outer sheath.

- It is EMI immune with high security.

- Network interconnection devices

  o   Repeaters

  - These are simple devices that raise the voltage of the electrical signal to extend the distance of the cable length.

  - They operate at the Physical layer of the OSI model.

  o   Bridges

  - These link separate network segments to form a single, cohesive, and transparent organizational information base.

  - They operate at the Data Link layer of the OSI model.

  o   Routers

  - These link dissimilar networks together.

  - They operate at the Network layer of the OSI model.

  o   Brouters

  - These are hybrid devices that route data transmissions that utilize *routed* protocols and use bridge-type links for those data transmissions that do not define a routing protocol.

  - They operate at the Network layer.

    o   Gateways

- These are the primary link between heterogeneous environments, such as PC-based LANs, and host environments, such as Systems Network Architecture (SNA).

- They operate at all seven layers of the OSI model.

- Network adapter cards

  These provide the hardware interface for the data-link protocols.

Course Reference Material

Manual

- Chapter 11
- Chapter 12
- Chapter 13

Digital Video

- Networking Fundamentals
- The OSI Model

Challenge! Interactive

- Basic Networking

Module 2
Exam 220-202: A+ Operating System (OS) Technologies

DOMAIN 1.0 OS FUNDAMENTALS

Exam Criteria

1.1 Identify the operating system's functions, structure, and major system files to navigate the operating system and how to get to needed technical information.

Points to Remember

Operating System Functions

- User interface

  Some operating systems, such as DOS, are controlled using a command-line interface. Other operating systems, such as Windows, are controlled using a graphical interface.

- Application management

  Windows operating systems must manage multiple applications at once, making sure that each application has the necessary resources available to function.

- File management

  If an application needs to retrieve or store data to a drive, the application must submit the request to the operating system.

- Hardware management

  The operating system is responsible for controlling all hardware devices within a computer system.

Online Help

- Windows 9x/2000 help system

  The Windows help system is easily accessed by choosing **Help** from the Windows **Start** menu.

- Microsoft TechNet

  TechNet is a service that provides in-depth *how-to* technical information on how to deploy, maintain, and support Microsoft products and operating systems.

  http://www.microsoft.com/technet

- Microsoft Knowledge Base

  The Microsoft Knowledge Base is a searchable database of more than 35,000 technical documents maintained by Microsoft that detail bugs, known issues, and answers to questions about Microsoft products.

  http://search.support.microsoft.com

- Company Web sites

  Many companies have their own product knowledge bases. Like Microsoft's Knowledge Base, these sites document bugs, common issues, and answers to questions regarding a company's products.

- Web search engines
  o http://www.yahoo.com
  o http://www.lycos.com
  o http://www.search.com
  o http://www.deja.com/usenet

Windows 95/98 System Files

- Io.sys, Msdos.sys, and Command.com
  o In MS-DOS-based systems, the Io.sys, Msdos.sys, and Command.com files are hidden binary files that are located in the root directory of the boot drive and are loaded when a computer is first turned on.
  o In Windows 9x, the Io.sys file performs the basic functions of both the DOS Io.sys and the DOS Msdos.sys files.

- Config.sys

  The Config.sys file contains commands relating to hardware, such as the memory, printer, mouse, keyboard, and disk drives present in your computer.

- Autoexec.bat

  This is a batch file used to customize the look of your computer, automatically start applications, and determine the operating characteristics of your hardware.

- Win.ini

  The Win.ini file is used to store information regarding the configuration and behavior of the Windows environment.

- System.ini

  The System.ini file is for storing information for device drivers, how DOS applications are handled, and internal Windows settings.

- NTLDR

  NTLDR is the operating system loader. In a multiboot system, it will be used to start the other operating systems. It is a hidden, read-only, system file that is located in the root of the boot drive.

- Bootsect.dos

  This file contains the boot sector of any operating system that was on the hard drive previous to installing Windows NT.

- Boot.ini

  The Boot.ini files controls the ability to boot to more than one operating system on a single computer. The Boot.ini file is a hidden, read-only text file stored in the root of the system partition.

FAT32

- File Allocation Table (FAT) history
  FAT organizes storage space on a hard drive. The FAT knows which cluster contains each piece of data.

- FAT32 features

  o FAT32 uses a partition as large as 2,047 GB and supports up to a 2-TB drive.

  o It uses smaller cluster sizes (4 KB on 8-GB or less drives) to use FAT32 disk space more efficiently (up to a 20% increase). The drive may gain hundreds of megabytes of free space when converted to FAT32.

  o It is more stable because a FAT32 drive can store a backup of critical data structures.

  o FAT32 can increase the speed applications load (up to 50% faster).

  o It uses these Microsoft disk utilities:

    - Format

    - Fdisk

    - Defrag

    - MS-DOS and Windows ScanDisk

    They have been converted to work with Windows 98 under FAT32.

  o FAT32 uses long filenames when supported by applications. The 8-character MS-DOS filename requirement no longer exists.

  o It can open a file nearly 4 GB in size.

- Comparing FAT32 and FAT16

FAT16	FAT32
MS-DOS, Windows 3.x, Windows 95, Windows 98, Windows NT, OS/2, and UNIX support FAT16.	FAT16's boot sector is stored in a sector only in one location. If that sector becomes corrupt, the computer may not be able to boot.
If the computer's drive is less than 256 MB, then FAT16 is very efficient regarding speed and storage.	If the computer's drive is greater than 512 MB, then FAT32 is much more efficient regarding speed and storage.
Many disk utilities have been developed based on FAT16.	The Microsoft set of disk utilities, including Format, Fdisk, Defrag, and ScanDisk for Windows and MS-DOS, have been converted to work well with FAT32. Microsoft is working with vendors to upgrade their FAT16 disk utilities to FAT32.

FAT16	FAT32
DriveSpace 3 can be used to compress FAT16 drives.	DriveSpace 3 cannot be used to compress FAT32 drives.
FAT16 stores 2 bytes per cluster in the FAT.	FAT32 stores 4 bytes per cluster in the FAT.

Drive Size	FAT16 Cluster Size	FAT32 Cluster Size
260 to 511 MB	8 KB	Not supported
512 to 1,023 MB	16 KB	4 KB
1,024 KB to 2 GB	32 KB	4 KB
2 to 8 GB	Not supported	4 KB
8 to 16 GB	Not supported	8 KB
16 to 32 GB	Not supported	16 KB
Greater than 32 GB	Not supported	32 KB

Navigating Window 95/98

- Control Panel

  There are three different ways to access the Control Panel. You can select the My Computer icon, use the **Start** menu and choose **Settings**, or select **Run** from the **Start** menu and type "CONTROL".

- Network Neigborhood

  The Network Neighborhood icon appears on your desktop when a network is available to your PC. When opened, this object displays all members of your workgroup as well as the entire network that is accessible.

- Windows Explorer

  - As you explore the contents of your local hard drive, you may point at an object and click your right mouse button to reveal a context-sensitive menu. This menu varies according to the object you have selected; you may have options such as **Open, Send To, Cut, Copy, Test, Configure**, and **Install**.

  - Due to the document-centric nature of Windows, you only need to locate the file that you wish to view and Windows will open up any associated applications for you.

  - The **Find** option on the **Start** menu allows you to search for either files or other computers on a network.

Memory Fundamentals

- Conventional memory

  o   The first 640 KB of system memory is commonly called *conventional memory.*

  o   It is used to load the DOS command processor, memory resident programs (TSRs), and DOS-based device drivers.

- Upper Memory Area (UMA)

  o   This is located between 640 KB and 1 MB.

  o   It contains the ROM BIOS, device controller ROM, and video controller ROM and RAM.

  o   Shadow RAM uses this memory area to shadow the ROM BIOS instructions, and hardware devices can store their program code here.

  o   When supporting expanded memory, it will also contain the expanded memory page frames.

- Upper Memory Blocks (UMBs)

  UMBs are free areas within the UMA. UMBs can be used to contain device drivers and memory resident programs (TSRs).

- Expanded Memory Specification (EMS)

  Expanded memory uses an expanded memory card placed in an expansion slot. It is basically just a card with memory chips on it.

- Extended Memory Specification (XMS)

  Memory above 1 MB (1,024 KB) is called *extended memory*. This is physically limited to 16 MB for 80286 microprocessors and 4 GB for 80386 and above microprocessors.

- High Memory Area (HMA)

  o   This is commonly used for loading DOS components but may be used for a different memory resident program.

  o   Only one program at a time may reside in the HMA.

- MEM

  The **MEM** command provides information about system memory such as the amount in use and the amount available.

Windows 98 Memory Management

- Virtual memory

  The term *virtual memory* means that in the Windows 98 operating system, more memory can be allocated than physically exists on the computer.

- Memory paging

  The area between 4 MB and 2 GB in the virtual memory layout contains Win32-based applications. This area is partitioned into equal blocks, or pages.

- Virtual memory swap file

  o A swap file allows free disk space to be used to store data that is loaded into memory.

  o To change the virtual memory settings:

  - Launch Control Panel from My Computer.

  - Launch the System utility and display the **Performance** tab.

  - Click on **Virtual Memory**.

- Memory Manager

  The Memory Manager information is displayed in the System Monitor   The System Monitor is a optional component of Windows 9x. To install it, go to Add/Remove Programs, click on the **Windows Setup** tab, and select it from the System Tools category.

DOS Commands

- Internal DOS commands

  o The Command.com file is responsible for interpreting what we type at the command line. It also contains the DOS internal commands.

  o Some commonly used DOS internal commands and their functions are listed in the following table.

DIR	Lists files in the current directory
CD	Changes to a different directory
COPY	Copies files
RD	Removes a directory
DEL	Deletes a file
REN	Renames a file
DATE	Displays or changes the date

TIME	Displays or changes the time
VER	Displays the operating system version
MD	Creates a directory
CLS	Clears the screen

- The command prompt

    o   The command prompt lets you know that the operating system is ready for a
        command to be typed.

    o   The **PROMPT** command can be executed from the command line or as part
        of the Autoexec.bat system configuration file. The typical prompt is created
        by typing the following and pressing *ENTER*:

        PROMPT=PG

- The Directory Listing (**DIR**) command

    The **DIR** command searches the desired path and displays the files and
    subdirectories found along with the date and time stamps for each, the size of each
    in bytes, the total space used for the files and subdirectories, and the total space
    available on the current drive.

        DIR [drive:][path][filename]

- The Change Directory (**CD**) command

        CD [/D] [drive:][path]

- The Make Directory (**MD** or **MKDIR**) command

        MKDIR [drive:]path
        MD [drive:]path

- The Remove Directory (**RD** or **RMDIR**) command

        RMDIR [/S] [/Q] [drive:]path
        RD [/S] [/Q] [drive:]path

- The **DELTREE** command

    While **RD** will only delete empty directories, the **DELTREE** command will delete
    an entire directory and its subdirectories and files with one command.

- The Rename (**REN**) command
  - o This allows you to change the name of a file without changing its contents. Any name that you give a file can be changed with the Rename command:

    ```
    REN drive_letter:path\filename newfilename
    ```
  - o There are rules to be followed when naming files. DOS places a limit on the length of filenames. The name itself can be up to 8 characters in length, followed by an optional 3-character extension. Windows increases the maximum length to 250 characters.

- The Delete (**DEL**) command

  ```
  DEL drive_letter:path\filename
  ```

- The **COPY** command

  This is used to copy files from one disk drive to another or from one directory to another:

  ```
  COPY source_drive_letter:path\filename
       destination_drive_letter:path\filename
  ```

- The **XCOPY** command

  This can be used to copy large groups of files:

  ```
  XCOPY source [destination]
  ```

- The **MOVE** command

  ```
  MOVE drive_letter:path\filename new_drive_letter:path
  ```

- The **ATTRIB** command

  ```
  ATTRIB [+R | -R] [+A | -A ] [+S | -S] [+H | -H] [[drive:] [path]
     filename]
  ```

Attribute	Use with Attribute On
Archive (+/- A)	Files are to be backed up.
Read-Only (+/- R)	Files cannot be modified or erased.
Hidden (+/- H)	Files will not appear in the directory.
System (+/- S)	Files are read-only and hidden.

Course Reference Material

Manual

- Chapter 1
- Chapter 4
  - Windows 95/98 System Files
  - Windows 2000 System Files
  - Navigating Windows 95/98
- Chapter 5
  - The FAT32 File System
- Chapter 7
  - Memory Fundamentals
  - Windows 98 Memory Management
- Chapter 8
  - DOS Commands

Digital Video

- Navigating Windows 98
- Navigating Windows 2000

NEXTSim

- Operating System Orientation
  - Create a Shortcut to a Network Server
  - Use Windows Explorer to Find a File
  - Change the Folder Options to Show All Files
  - Customize the Start Menu
- Software Management
  - Use the Command Prompt to Manage Files and Directories

Challenge! Interactive

- OS Fundamentals

Exam Criteria

1.2   Identify basic concepts and procedures for creating, viewing, and managing files, directories, and disks. This includes procedures for changing file attributes and the ramifications of those changes (for example, security issues).

Points to Remember

- Partitioning
  - o   A partition is the process of dividing a hard drive into logical drives.
  - o   Windows will assign each partition a separate drive letter, such as C:\ and D:\.
- Partition types
  - o   When a partition is created, you must choose a file system for that partition to use.
  - o   File systems that are supported by Microsoft operating systems are described in the following table.

Partition Types	Operating Systems Supporting the Partition Type
FAT16	MS-DOS versions 5.0 and higher and all versions of Windows
FAT32	Windows 95 OEM Service Release 2 (OSR2), Windows 98, and Windows 2000
NTFS	Windows NT and Windows 2000
HPFS	OS/2 operating system and Windows NT 3.5x

  - o   To determine how a Windows 98 system is currently partitioned:
    - Open a command prompt or the Run dialog.
    - Type "FDISK" and press *ENTER.*
    - Select the **Display Partition Information** option. The Display Partition Information screen appears.
    - The disk space displayed represents the uncompressed drive size. If compression software has been used on a drive, it will not be indicated. If software other than Microsoft was used to compress a drive, the drive may not be listed at all.

- Deleting a partition or logical drive

  o The Fdisk utility can be used to remove MS-DOS partitions, logical drives, an extended MS-DOS partition, or the primary MS-DOS partition.

  o When Fdisk is used to delete an MS-DOS partition, a logical drive, an extended MS-DOS partition, or the primary MS-DOS partition, all data on the partition will be deleted. All applications and data currently on these drives should be backed up prior to deleting a partition.

- Creating a partition or logical drive

  o Once all DOS partitions and/or logical DOS partitions have been deleted, a Primary DOS partition should be created.

  o To make the Primary DOS partition active:

    - Run **Fdisk**.

    - Press *2* for Set active partition, then press *ENTER*.

    - Follow the instructions on the screen.

- Converting to FAT32

  o A partition is converted to FAT32 using the Drive Converter (FAT32) **Wizard.**

  o Drive Converter (FAT32) in protected mode

     Launch Drive Converter (FAT32) from the **Start | Accessories | System Tools** menu. This Drive Converter (FAT32) application is Cvt1.exe and is located in the Windows directory.

  o Drive Converter (FAT32) in real mode

     The Drive Converter (FAT32) application is Cvt.exe. It can be typed at a command prompt to start the conversion.

- Compression

  o A compressed drive is one that has a Compressed Volume File (CVF) created by compression software.

  o DriveSpace 3 is included with Windows 98. It can be used to compress FAT16 drives.

- Drive properties

  o In Windows 98, information about compression is available in the drive's Properties dialog.

  o To view a drive's properties, launch My Computer, right-click on the desired drive, and select **Properties**.

- DriveSpace 3

  To run the DriveSpace 3 program, launch **DriveSpace** from the **Start |
  Programs | Accessories | System Tools** menu, click on **Run DriveSpace** from the
  Advanced Properties for *Drive* screen, or type "drvspace" at the Run dialog.

- Hard drive optimization

  Increased efficiency and speed can be the result of intensive hard drive
  maintenance. Windows 98 includes three utilities that improve hard drive access
  performance by reorganizing clusters optimally, finding and correcting errors on
  the hard disk, and removing unnecessary files to increase disk space.

- Disk Defragmenter

  o   Fragmentation occurs over time as data is written to and read from the hard
      disk. The data starts being stored in clusters that are not next to each other, so
      it takes longer for the computer to read the data.

  o   Launch **Disk Defragmenter** from the **Start | Programs | Accessories | System
      Tools** menu or type "defrag" in the Run dialog. From the Drive Selection
      dialog, click on **Settings** to verify your settings.

- ScanDisk

  o   The ScanDisk program, Scandisk.exe, is an application that can examine a
      hard disk for errors (both physical and logical).

  o   Once ScanDisk finds an error, it can also repair it.

  o   ScanDisk can be run by launching it from the **Start | Programs | Accessories |
      System Tools** menu; by opening My Computer, right-clicking on the desired
      drive, displaying the **Tools** tab, and clicking on **Check Now** (this screen also
      provides information about the last time the drive was checked); or by typing
      "scandisk" at the Run dialog.

- Disk Cleanup

  The Disk Cleanup tool enables you to quickly acquire more disk space by
  checking and deleting the same files you would manually (such as those in the
  Recycle Bin, Temporary files, and Temporary Internet files).

- Using Microsoft Backup for Windows 98

  One of the most important maintenance tasks that should be performed regularly
  is a backup of the data on any local hard drives.

- About Microsoft Backup for Windows 98

  Microsoft Backup for Windows 98 provides the ability to back up files to disk,
  tape, parallel devices, IDE/ATAPI, and SCSI backup devices.

- Installing Microsoft Backup

  To install Microsoft Backup:

  o Launch Add/Remove Programs from the Control Panel.

  o Display the **Windows Setup** tab.

  o Select the System Tools component and click on **Details**.

  o Select Backup and click on **OK**. Click on **OK** to close Add/Remove Program Properties. The necessary files are copied from the Windows 98 source. A shortcut is added to **Start | Programs | Accessories | System Tools**.

- Creating a new backup job

  o Open the Microsoft Backup application by launching **Backup** from the **Start | Programs | Accessories | System Tools** menu.

  o If the backup had been completed with no errors, a Job Report is also created and provides information about the time of the job and the bytes processed.

- Running a backup job manually

  To run a backup job manually instead of through Scheduled Tasks:

  o Launch **Backup** from the **Start | Programs | Accessories | System Tools** menu.

  o Enable the **Open an existing backup job** option button and click on **OK**.

  o Select a backup job from the list and click on **Open**.

  o Make sure the backup medium is ready and click on **Start**.

  o Click on **OK** when the Operation completed dialog appears.

- Scheduling a backup job using the Scheduled Task Wizard

  The Scheduled Task Wizard allows you to schedule backup jobs for convenient times.

- Backup job options

  There are several options regarding the backup. To reach these options, click on **Options** from the main Microsoft Backup screen or select **Options** from the **Job** menu.

- Restoring files from a backup

  o Launch **Backup** from the **Start | Programs | Accessories | System Tools** menu.

  o Run **Restore Wizard** from the **Tools** menu.

Using Microsoft Backup for Windows 2000

- Local vs. network backups
  - The Windows Backup utility supports both network and local backups.
  - Local backups are run individually on each system.
  - Network backups let you back up data from multiple systems from one central location.
- Backup media

  Backup media is another important consideration. Windows 2000 supports backup to disk or removable media (such as a writeable CD-ROM or an Iomega Zip drive).
- Backup types
  - Normal/full

    All selected files are backed up. Each file's Archive attribute is reset to identify that the file has been backed up.
  - Copy

    All selected files are backed up, but the Archive bit is not reset on any of the files. There is nothing to indicate that the files have been backed up recently.
  - Differential

    Only those files whose Archive bit is set (needing backup) are backed up by a differential backup. The Archive bit is not reset on the files.
  - Incremental

    This is similar to a differential backup in that only those files that the Archive bit is set on are backed up. The difference is that an incremental backup resets the Archive bit on the files it backs up.
  - Daily

    Only files changed today (modified today) are backed up. The Archive bit is not reset on the files.
- Backup utility

  To launch the Backup utility, run **Start | Programs | Accessories | System Tools | Backup**.
- Backup options

  You can display the Backup options pages by running **Tools | Options**. The backup options set default backup settings for the utility.

- Backup Log options

    The Backup Log options determine the type of backup log that is generated each time a backup runs. The available log options are:

    o   Detailed

    This will log all information about the backup.

    o   Summary

    Only key information about the backup is logged.

    o   None

    No backup log is created.

- Using Encrypting File System (EFS)

    o   Data encryption

    - Windows 2000 provides a way of protecting data through EFS. EFS is only supported on NTFS volumes.

    - EFS uses public key authentication to ensure that only the user who creates a file is able to open it.

    o   Recovery agents

    The recovery agent is specified through the Encrypted Data Recovery Policy (EDRP).

- Encryption guidelines

    o   You can encrypt most files that you want to protect, but there are some restrictions. You cannot encrypt the following:

    - Files on a FAT partition

    - A volume's root folder

    - Compressed files

    - System files

    o   Encrypted data is protected during backup and restore.

- Managing encryption and decryption

    Files can be encrypted through Windows Explorer or through the use of the Cipher command-line utility.

- Windows Explorer

    Display the file's properties pages. Click on the **Advanced** button on the file's General properties sheet. Place a check in the **Encrypt contents to secure data** checkbox and click on **OK** to encrypt the file.

- Cipher
  - You can also manage encryption using the **Cipher** command. The **Cipher** command lets you:
    - Encrypt files or folders.
    - Decrypt files or folders.
    - Display the encryption attribute status of files or folders.
  - The syntax for running **Cipher** is as follows:
    ```
    CIPHER [/E|/D] [/S:directory]
    ```
- Managing data compression
  - Data compression is an NTFS volume-specific feature.
  - You can choose to compress a file, the contents of a folder, or an entire volume.
- Data compression overview
  - Compression provides a means of storing more data in less space.
  - Compression is only supported on NTFS volumes. It is supported on both NTFS version 4 and NTFS version 5 volumes, with the same compression bit algorithm.
  - Windows 2000 disk compression is not compatible with Windows 9x DriveSpace compression due to differences in the compression algorithm used. Windows 2000 cannot read drives compressed with DriveSpace.
- Automatic compression/decompression

  A compression bit is used to determine whether a folder's contents or an individual file should be compressed. If a folder's compression bit is set, all files written to that folder will be compressed automatically.

- File move and copy

  When a compressed file or folder is moved or copied, it is first decompressed. Whether it is recompressed depends on its destination, as outlined below:

  - Copying a file or folder to a new location on the same NTFS volume

    The file will inherit the compression state of the destination folder, either compressed or uncompressed.

  - Moving a file or folder to a new location on the same NTFS volume

    The file or folder retains its original compression state.

  - Copying a file or folder to a different NTFS volume

    The file or folder inherits its destination folder's compression state.

o   Moving a file or folder to a different NTFS volume

The file or folder inherits its destination folder's compression state.

o   Copying/moving a file or folder to a FAT volume

Since FAT volumes do not support Windows 2000 (or Windows NT) compression, the file or folder will be stored as uncompressed.

- Managing compression

Some general guidelines for efficient use of data compression include:

o   Compress files that benefit most from compression.

o   Don't compress files that are already compressed.

o   Don't compress files that frequently change.

- Managing compression with Windows Explorer

To have Windows Explorer provide a visual cue for compressed files and folders, run **Tools | Folder Options**.

- **Compact** command

The **Compact** command-line command can also be used for managing disk compression. The general syntax for this command is as follows:

```
COMPACT [/C|/U] [/S[:path_name]]
```

Course Reference Material

Manual

- Chapter 5
  o   The FAT32 File System
  o   Hard Drive Optimization
  o   Using Microsoft Backup for Windows 98
- Chapter 6
  o   Using Windows 2000 Backup Utility
  o   Using Encrypting File System
  o   Managing Data Compression

NEXTSim

- Windows 98 Disk and File Management
  - ○ Convert FAT16 Drive to FAT32 Using Drive Converter
  - ○ Run System Utilities for Hard Disk Management
  - ○ Install and Use Microsoft Backup
- Windows 2000 Disk and File Management
  - ○ Use Microsoft Backup to Back Up Files
  - ○ Encrypt Files

Challenge! Interactive

- OS Fundamentals

Exam Criteria

1.3 Identify the procedures for basic disk management.

Points to Remember

Windows 2000 Disk Management

- Primary vs. extended partitions

  There are two types of partitions: primary partitions and extended partitions. A primary partition is a hard disk division that is formatted with a file system and has a unique drive letter. An extended partition is a hard disk division that can be further subdivided into multiple logical drives, each with its own drive letter and file system.

- Boot and system partitions
  - ○ System partition

    The system partition is the partition used to boot Windows 2000. It will contain the hardware-specific files needed to load the operating system, including NTLDR. The system partition must be a primary partition and must be marked as active.

o   Boot partition

   The boot partition contains the operating system files needed to launch and run Windows 2000. The boot partition can be any logical drive or partition.

o   The boot partition and system partition can, but are not required to, be the same partition.

- Disk Management Snap-in

   o   The Disk Management Snap-in is available through the Computer Management tool.

   o   You can use it to view and manage physical drives, logical drives, partitions, and volumes.

- Windows 2000 file systems

   o   Windows 2000 supports the following file systems:

      - FAT16

      - FAT32

      - NTFS

   o   The Universal Disk Format (UDF) is new with Windows 2000 and provides support for read-only DVD media.

- File Allocation Table (FAT) file systems

   o   Windows 2000 supports two versions of the FAT file system: FAT16 and FAT32. Support for FAT16 on Windows 2000 is the same as on MS-DOS, Windows 3.x, and Windows 9x; support for FAT32 is the same as on Windows 95 OSR2 and Windows 98.

   o   FAT16

      - Under FAT16, the hard disk is formatted with 512-byte sectors.

      - The operating system allocates file space based on clusters, or groups of sectors.

      - The default cluster size is based on the partition size.

      - The FAT16 file system can support partitions up to 4 GB under Windows 2000.

      - DOS and Windows 9x systems using FAT16 can only recognize FAT partitions that are no larger than 2 GB.

- o FAT32
  - • FAT32 partitions created by Windows 2000 can be no larger than 32 GB.
  - • File allocation is managed through clusters.
  - • The maximum partition size is determined by the cluster size.
- o Using FAT
  - • You should use FAT16 or FAT32 when backward compatibility is required or when Windows 2000 Professional must be installed to dual boot with another operating system.
  - • If some disk partitions are formatted as FAT and others as NTFS on a dual-boot system, the NTFS partitions will only be visible when the system is booted to Windows NT or Windows 2000. When booted to other operating systems, the drive letters will be assigned as if the NTFS partitions did not exist. This can cause confusion and make users believe files are missing.
- • NT File System (NTFS)
  - o NTFS allows a system to support NTFS-specific features, such as local access permissions, recovery, disk compression, and encryption through EFS.
  - o At least one NTFS volume is required on each domain controller in an Active Directory domain.
  - o Space is allocated based on clusters. The cluster size also determines the maximum volume size.
  - o The practical limit of an NTFS partition is 2 TB.
- • Converting to NTFS
  ```
  CONVERT d: /FS:NTFS /v
  ```
  Replace *d*: with the drive ID of the drive to be converted.
- • Managing basic storage

  Basic storage is the industry standard for hard disk storage.
- • Basic storage key points
  - o Disk organization
    - • Basic disks are organized around partitions.
    - • A partition defines a unit of disk storage.

- Two types of partitions are supported:
  - o Primary partitions
  - o Extended partitions

    An extended partition can be further subdivided into logical drives.

  o Operating system support

    Basic disks are supported by MS-DOS, Microsoft Windows *X* (all versions), Windows NT (all versions), and Windows 2000.

- Removable storage device restrictions

  The following are some special restrictions placed on removable storage devices:

  o Removable storage devices must be configured as basic disks.

  o Removable storage devices support primary partitions only (no extended partitions or logical drives).

  o A primary partition on a removable storage device cannot be marked as active (system partition).

- Basic disk configurations

  o On Windows 2000 Professional, a basic disk supports the following:

    - Primary partition

      o One important reason for defining a primary partition is so it can be used as a bootable partition (system partition).

      o You identify the bootable partition by marking it as active.

    - Extended partition

      A hard disk can only have one extended partition, but an extended partition can be divided into multiple logical drives.

    - Volume set

      o In a volume set, multiple partitions are logically joined as a single logical disk.

      o Regular backups are critical when using volume sets; loss of any partition in the volume set means loss of all data in the volume.

    - Stripe set

      Data is striped across the disks; that is, data is alternately written to each of the drives in the stripe set.

- A primary partition on a single drive or a mirror set can be configured as bootable (system partition). You cannot boot from an extended partition, volume set, stripe set, or stripe set with parity.

- Adding disks

  - If you are adding permanent storage media, such as an internal hard disk, you will typically have to shut off the system before adding the disk and reboot after.

  - The system (and Disk Manager) should recognize the disk automatically.

  - If you are adding a removable storage disk subsystem, you will have to tell Disk Manager that a new disk has been added.

  - Run **Action | Rescan Disks** to have Disk Manager look for new disks.

- Creating partitions

  To create a partition (primary or extended), right-click on unpartitioned disk space and run **Create Partition**.

- Creating logical drives

  - Select unassigned space in an extended partition.

  - Right-click on the partition and run **Create Logical Drive**.

- Deleting partitions and logical drives

  To delete a partition or logical drive, right-click on it and run **Delete Partition** or **Delete Logical Drive**.

- Managing dynamic disks

  - When you configure a disk as a dynamic disk, a single disk partition is created that includes the entire disk.

  - Dynamic disks are organized around disk volumes.

  - A disk volume can be made up of all or part of one or more physical hard disks.

- Setting the storage type

  - You can change storage types through the Disk Management Snap-in.

  - You should always back up a disk before changing its storage type.

- Basic disk to dynamic disk

  Right-click on the drive in the Disk Management Snap-in and run **Upgrade to Dynamic Disk**.

- Dynamic disk to basic disk
    - o First delete any volumes that are on the disk.
    - o Right-click on the disk and run **Revert To Basic Disk.**
    - o Unlike upgrading a drive to make it a dynamic disk, reverting back to a basic disk is a destructive operation. Be sure to back up any data before reverting the disk.
- Dynamic disk configurations
    - o Simple volumes

      A simple volume includes disk space from one hard disk only.
    - o Spanned volumes

      A spanned volume can include space from up to 32 physical hard disks.
    - o Striped volumes
        - Up to 32 physical hard disks can be included in a striped volume.
        - Striped volumes do not provide fault tolerance.

Course Reference Material

Manual

- Chapter 5
- Chapter 6

NEXTSim

- Windows 98 Disk and File Management
    - o Run System Utilities for Hard Disk Management
    - o Schedule Tasks in Windows 98
    - o Install and Use Microsoft Backup
- Windows 2000 Disk and File Management
    - o Use Microsoft Backup to Back Up Files
    - o Use Microsoft Backup to Restore Files

Challenge! Interactive

- OS Fundamentals

DOMAIN 2.0 INSTALLATION, CONFIGURATION, AND UPGRADING

Exam Criteria

2.1   Identify the procedures for installing Windows 9x and Windows 2000 for bringing the software to a basic operational level.

Points to Remember

Installing Windows 2000

- Windows 95 installation requirements
    - Intel (or compatible) 386DX or higher processor
    - 4 MB of memory (8 MB is recommended)
    - VGA-compatible video adapter
    - High-density floppy disk drive
    - Hard disk drive
- Recommended hardware includes:
    - Mouse or other pointing device
    - CD-ROM drive
    - Fax/modem
- Windows 95 supports five methods of installation:
    - CD-ROM
    - Administrative (to network)
    - Workstation (from network)
    - Floppy disks
    - Batch
- Starting Windows 95 Setup

    To start the Setup, run **Setup.exe** from the Windows 95 CD.

- Windows 95 Setup Wizard options

  The Windows 95 Setup Wizard provides four installation methods:

  o Typical

  o Portable

  o Compact

  o Custom

- Steps in Windows 95 Setup

  Setup in Windows 95 is more automated than Setup in Windows 3.1 and is divided into the following four steps:

  o Setup information and PC hardware detection

     Setup will compile system information and attempt to detect installed hardware.

  o Configuration questions

     Setup will query the user about system configuration.

  o Copying component files

     Setup will determine which files are required for the specific system configuration and copy them to your hard disk.

  o Restart and final configuration

     Setup restarts your PC using the Windows 95 operating system and performs final configuration tasks.

- Hardware detection phase

  o During the hardware detection phase, Setup analyzes installed system components, searches for installed hardware devices, and detects any connected peripherals.

  o During the detection process, Windows 95 prompts the user to indicate whether certain devices are present. These devices are as follows:

     • Sound cards

     • SCSI devices

     • Network adapters

     • Proprietary CD-ROMs

- First-time run

  Final configuration takes place after you start Windows 95 for the first time. This configuration includes the following:

  o Creation of the password list occurs when you enter the initial password.

  o The **Start** menu is configured and any existing Windows 3.1 Program Groups are converted to folders.

  o Windows 95 sets up printers.

  o Time zone information is entered.

  o The Windows 95 Tour is enabled, and you are asked if you would like to take the tour.

Installing Windows 98

- Windows 98 system requirements

  o 486 DX2, 66-MHz processor (or higher)

  o 16 MB of RAM

  o 110 MB of hard disk space (for a local installation)

  o VGA monitor (or better)

  o Mouse or other pointing device

- Optional hardware

  o Modem

  o Network adapter

  o CD-ROM

  o Audio card and speakers

  o DVD-ROM and decoder card

  o Digital camera and/or scanner

  o Additional monitor(s) and video card(s)

- Hard disk requirements

  Windows 98 Setup must install the Windows 98 operating system on a File Allocation Table (FAT) partition located on the hard disk.

- Operating system requirements

Windows 98 can be installed on a formatted hard disk or as an upgrade over MS-DOS, Windows 3.1, Windows for Workgroups, or Windows 95. Windows 98 can also be installed as a dual-boot operating system with Windows NT, Windows 2000, or OS/2.

- Creating a boot disk
  - o   To create a DOS boot diskette, do the following:
    1.   Bring up a DOS prompt.
    2.   Insert a formatted diskette and type "sys A:". Or insert an unformatted diskette and type "format /s A:".
    3.   Verify that Command.com is on the diskette.
    4.   Copy Format.com, Fdisk.exe, Sys.com, Autoexec.bat, Config.sys, and any required device driver files onto the diskette.
  - o   To create a Windows 95 boot diskette, do the following:
    1.   Create a Windows 95 boot disk by launching Add/Remove Programs from the Control Panel.
    2.   Display the **Startup Disk** tab.
    3.   Click on **Create Disk**.
    4.   Follow the instructions on your screen.
    5.   Verify that the diskette contains the Fdisk.exe and Format.com files before proceeding.

- Reformatting the hard drive
  - o   Before reformatting the hard drive, make sure you have a copy of all files or applications that you will want to reinstall once the new operating system has been installed. Make sure you also have all required device drivers, such as the CD-ROM drivers, available.
  - o   To reformat the hard drive, do the following:
    1.   Make sure that the boot disk is in the drive. Restart the computer. When the computer is powered up, a cursor will appear at the A:\> prompt or you may have to type "A:". Then press *ENTER* to reach the A:\ drive.
    If the floppy drive is a letter other than A:\, type that letter instead.

    NOTE: *Remember, Fdisk deletes all information from your hard drive!*

    2.   Type "FDISK" and press **ENTER**.

- Installing Windows 98 on a formatted drive

  The following instructions should be used when installing Windows 98 on a formatted hard drive:

  1. Insert the Windows 98 CD into the CD-ROM drive or insert Setup Disk 1 from the Setup disk set into the floppy drive.

  2. At the command prompt, change the path to the CD or Setup disk. For example, the CD-ROM drive may be D: or the floppy drive may be A:.

  3. Launch **Setup.exe**.

  4. ScanDisk starts, then the Setup Wizard appears.

- Additional installation options

  You also have your choice of installation sources and methods. These include the following:

  o Shared installation to a file server

     Installation of Windows 98 to a network server allows you to set up Windows 98 on workstations and share Windows 98 system files.

  o Automated installations

     You can automate installation by using a logon script to run **Setup** from a batch script, allowing automatic installation to remote workstations.

  o Upgrade or maintenance installations

     After a successful Windows 98 installation, you can run **Setup** to verify and repair the existing installation.

  o Command-line switches

     Another installation variation is using command-line switches when starting **Setup.exe** from a DOS prompt. These switches modify the setup process so that it takes specified actions. To use a switch, type "setup" followed by a forward slash (/) and the switch. If there are multiple switches, type a forward slash in front of each one.

- The stages of Setup

  There are five stages in a successful Setup.

  o Preparing to run Windows 98 Setup

  o Collecting information about your computer

  o Copying Windows 98 files to your computer

  o Restarting your computer

  o Setting up hardware and finalizing settings

- Preparing to start Setup

To avoid potential problems, use the following check list.

	Decide on the best way to install Windows 98: • DOS prompt • Windows 95 • Network-automated installation • Setup script
	Decide if you need to dual boot with another operating system.
	Decide which components will be installed.
	Make sure that your hardware meets the minimum requirements.
	Make sure that you have a FAT partition available with at least the minimum amount of disk space required available.
	Make sure you have a backup of all critical personal files, system configuration files, and applications.
	Make sure the network is functioning properly prior to installing Windows 98.
	Disable any anti-virus software.
	Disable any DOS applications.
	Make sure you have a boot diskette for your current operating system prior to starting the install.
	Make sure the MS-DOS version is 5.0 or greater if installing from DOS.

- Starting the Setup Wizard

To start the installation, run **Setup.exe** from your installation source.

- ScanDisk

Next, the Setup Wizard will scan your hard drive.

- Collecting information about your computer

  The following screens are displayed during this second stage:

  o License Agreement

  o Product Key

  o Select Directory

  o Checking Your System

  o Preparing Directory

  o Saving System Files

  o Setup Options

  o User Info

  o Windows Components

  o Location Setup for Web

  o Startup Disk

- Safe Recovery

  Windows 98 Setup collects information about setup actions that have been performed and what hardware has been detected. This information is stored in a log file. If Setup fails and is restarted, Setup can continue based on the information stored in the log file.

- Select Directory

  The default directory name is the same as the previous Windows version on the computer; it will be C:\WIN98 if you are installing on a newly formatted disk.

- Setup Options

  The Setup Options dialog prompts whether a **Typical, Portable, Compact,** or **Custom** installation should occur.

- Save System Files

  The Save System Files dialog asks if existing system files should be saved in order to uninstall Windows 98, if necessary, in the future. These files could take up to 50 MB of disk space.

- Startup Disk

  The next action is to create a startup disk.

- Copying Windows 98 files to your computer

  The third stage starts the Windows 98 file transfer.

- Restarting your computer

  After the file transfer is complete, the fourth stage, Restarting your computer, begins. The Restarting your computer listing is highlighted on the left of the screen, and the Restart dialog appears.

- Setting up hardware and finalizing settings

  o The fifth and final stage of the Setup is setting up the hardware. Windows 98 Setup analyzes the hardware information collected and sets up Plug and Play devices and any legacy hardware devices. The computer performs another restart (automatically or when **Restart Now** is clicked on). When the computer reboots, the hardware configurations are set up, then the following system settings are configured:

    - Time Zone (In a DOS install, you may be required to select the appropriate time zone.)

    - Control Panel

    - Programs on the **Start** menu

    - Windows Help

    - MS-DOS program settings

    - Tuning up Application Start

    - System configuration

  o The computer is then rebooted again and you are prompted for a Name and Password for existing networks and Windows.

- Custom installations

  o A custom installation uses a script (INF) file written in the Msbatch.inf format. The Batch utility is available to help you write this file.

  o The Batch program, Batch.exe, is located on your installation CD in the \Tools\Reskit\Batch directory.

  o To install the Batch program, open the Run dialog and type the following:
      `d:\tools\reskit\batch\setup.exe`
  NOTE: Drive d:\represents your CD-ROM drive letter.

  o With the Microsoft Batch 98 utility, you can:

    - Set up a new customized INF file.

    - Edit an existing INF file.

- Click on **Gather now** to create an INF file based on the computer's configuration.

- Use the compiled HTML help file.

- Automated installations

  Windows 98 Setup can occur automatically with a setup script, plus logon scripts, and user accounts on a network. Once the scripts are in place, you may install Windows 98 remotely using one of the following methods:

  o Create a network logon script that runs the Setup using the INF script when each user logs on.

  o Use an electronic mail message to allow a user to start Windows 98 Setup by clicking on a Setup object.

  o Use Microsoft Systems Management Server (SMS) to make Windows 98 Setup a mandatory job.

  o Use network management software provided by other vendors to automate the Setup process.

Installing Windows 2000

- Hardware requirements

System Hardware	Minimum Installation Requirement (Server)	Minimum Installation Requirement (Professional)
Processor	133-MHz Pentium	133-MHz Pentium
Memory	128 MB of RAM	64 MB of RAM
Disk space	671 MB of free disk space	620 MB of free disk space
Display	VGA monitor, minimum 640 x 480	VGA monitor, minimum 640 x 480

- Hardware compatibility

  The Setup program will report any potential conflicts it detects, but it is still best to check the Hardware Compatibility List (HCL). A copy of the HCL is located in the Support folder of the Installation CD-ROM. An up-to-date HCL can also be downloaded from the following location:

  http://www.microsoft.com/hcl

- Installation sources
  - o Installation CD-ROM
  - o Setup boot disks
  - o Shared network installation
- Installation CD-ROM

  Boot from CD-ROM
  - o You can boot directly from the Installation CD-ROM as long as it is supported by your CD-ROM drive and system BIOS.
  - o You may need to modify your BIOS configuration to allow the system to use the CD-ROM drive as a boot source.
- Setup boot disks

  The Windows 2000 Server Installation CD-ROM provides two utilities for creating Setup disks:
  - o Makeboot.exe

    This is the 16-bit version of the utility. Use this version when creating the disks on an MS-DOS or Windows 3.x system.
  - o Makebt32.exe

    This is the 32-bit version of the utility that runs on Windows 95, Windows 98, Windows NT, and Windows 2000.
- Shared network installation

  A shared network folder is commonly used as an installation source for unattended installations but can also be used for running attended installations as long as the destination system is able to access the source directory.
- Destination partition
  - o Windows 2000 Professional installation requires that you have at least 620 MB of free disk space on a disk partition that is located on a permanent hard disk.
  - o Windows 2000 Server requires that you have at least 671 MB of free disk space.

- File systems
  - ○ FAT16

    Partition size is limited to 2,048 MB, there is no local access security, and many Windows 2000 features such as disk quotas and disk encryption are not supported.

  - ○ FAT32

    If you choose to format a partition as FAT under Windows 2000 (or during Setup), partitions larger than 2,048 MB will be formatted as FAT32 automatically.

  - ○ NTFS

    NTFS is supported by Windows NT 3.51 and Windows NT 4.0. You will need to install to an NTFS partition if you want to support NTFS features such as local access security.

- Licensing options
  - ○ You must have a Client Access License (CAL) for each system that connects to a Windows 2000 Server system.
  - ○ Windows 2000 Server offers the following two options for managing CALs:
    - Per-server licensing
    - Per-seat licensing

- Windows 2000 Server components

  When installing Windows 2000 Server, you will be prompted to select the Windows 2000 Server components that you want to install:
  - ○ Accessories and utilities
  - ○ Certificate Services
  - ○ Indexing Service
  - ○ Internet Information Server (IIS) services
  - ○ Management and Monitoring Tools
  - ○ Message Queuing Services
  - ○ Networking services
  - ○ Other network file and print services
  - ○ Remote Installation Services (RIS)
  - ○ Remote storage

o   Script Debugger

o   Terminal Services

o   Terminal Services licensing

o   Windows media services

- Workgroup/domain membership

During installation, you will be prompted to join a workgroup or domain.

Course Reference Material

Manual

- Chapter 2
- Chapter 3

Digital Video

- Windows 98 Installation
- Windows 2000 Installation

NEXTSim

- Windows 95/98 Installation

  o   Upgrade Windows 95 to Windows 98

Challenge! Interactive

- Installation, Configuration, and Upgrading

Exam Criteria

2.2   Identify steps to perform an operating system upgrade.

Points to Remember

Updating an Existing Windows Installation to Windows 95

To install the upgrade version of Windows 95, you must have a previous version of Windows, Windows for Workgroups, or MS-DOS 3.1 or higher installed.

- Upgrade from Windows 3.x
  - o   The preferred method for running Windows 95 Setup is from within Windows 3.1 or Windows for Workgroups 3.11.
  - o   If MS-DOS, OS/2, Windows NT 3.x, or Windows 3.0 is installed, it is recommended that you run Setup from MS-DOS.
  - o   During Setup, Windows renames the Command.com, Config.sys, and Autoexec.bat files to Command.dos, Config.dos, and Autoexec.dos.
  - o   Before upgrading a PC to Windows 95, collect the following information:
    - Default username
    - Workstation name for network users
    - Workgroup name for network users
    - Domain name for Windows NT server domain members
    - Preferred server name for Novell NetWare environments
- Upgrade from MS-DOS and dual booting
  - o   Windows 95 supports dual booting between MS-DOS/Windows 3.x and Windows 95.
  - o   After installation, you must place the following entry in the Msdos.sys file:
    ```
    BootMulti=1
    ```
  - o   This will allow you to press *F8* during the Windows 95 Startup and select the option for starting the previous version of MS-DOS.
- Upgrading from a previous version of Windows 95

  If you are upgrading a workstation from a previous version of Windows 95, the update can be run from within Windows.

Updating an Existing Windows Installation to Windows 98

- Upgrading Windows 3.1 to Windows 98

  When upgrading from Windows 3.1, Windows 98 must be installed from the DOS prompt.

- Upgrading Windows for Workgroups to Windows 98

  When upgrading from Windows 3.1, Windows 98 must be installed from the DOS prompt.

- Upgrading Windows 95 to Windows 98

  o   The Windows 98 Setup application on the Windows 98 CD-ROM will run automatically when it is placed in the CD-ROM drive.

  o   Windows 98 cannot be installed into a shared Windows 95 or Windows 2000 folder.

- Installing Windows 98 with Windows 2000

  Windows 98 can be installed in combination with Windows 2000 only when Windows 2000 is dual booting with MS-DOS.

- Installing Windows 98 with OS/2

  o   OS/2 can optionally use the High Performance File System (HPFS) instead of the traditional File Allocation Table (FAT) for its directory structure.

  o   Windows 98 cannot be installed over HPFS.

  o   If the OS/2 system has a FAT partition available, Windows 98 can be installed.

  o   When installing Windows 98 on a computer running OS/2, the following notes apply:

    - You must install Windows 98 in a different directory.

    - Desktop or other settings used in OS/2 cannot be migrated to Windows 98.

    - Windows-based applications may have to be reinstalled to run under Windows 98.

    - You may need to have the OS/2 disk 1 available during Setup.

  o   Windows 98 Setup cannot be started from within OS/2 or OS/2 for Windows.

- Dual-boot installations

  o When installing Windows 98 on a Windows 2000 system, it is recommended that you create a Windows 2000 Emergency Repair Disk and back up any important data before you begin installing Windows 98.

  o If you do not have MS-DOS installed, creating the Emergency Repair Disk is not optional. You will need it after Windows 98 installation to enable dual boot.

  o To create an emergency repair disk, click on **Start | Programs | Accessories | System Tools** and click on the **Backup** option. This will open the Microsoft Backup program. The option to create an Emergency Repair Disk is on the **Tools** menu.

  o You cannot run the Windows 98 Setup program from within Windows 2000. You must start your system with MS-DOS.

Updating an Existing Windows Installation to Windows 2000

- Existing operating systems

  o You have the option of either upgrading the current operating system if you are running any of the following:

    - Windows NT 3.51 Server

    - Windows NT 4.0 Server

    - Windows NT 4.0 Terminal Server

  o Windows 2000 Professional can be installed over the following operating systems:

    - Windows 95

    - Windows 98

    - Windows NT Workstation 3.51

    - Windows NT Workstation 4.0

- AutoPlay (or run **Setup.exe**)

  As long as you haven't disabled AutoPlay, you will be prompted with the Windows 2000 Server Setup Wizard or Windows 2000 Professional Setup Wizard after inserting the Installation CD-ROM in a system running Windows 95, Windows 98, Windows NT, or Windows 2000. This is a convenient method to use when upgrading and installing on a system that already has an operating system installed.

- Setup executables

  There are three Setup executables. They are as follows:

  o   Winnt.exe

      Run to launch a clean install from MS-DOS or Windows 3.x.

  o   Winnt32.exe

      - For a clean install on Windows 95, Windows 98, Windows NT Workstation, or Windows NT Server

      - To upgrade Windows NT 3.51 Server, Windows NT 4.0 Server, or Windows NT 4.0 Terminal Server to Windows 2000 Server

      - To upgrade Windows 95, Windows 98, Windows NT Workstation 3.51, or Windows NT Workstation 4.0 to Windows 2000 Professional

  o   Setup.exe

      Run to launch **Winnt.exe** or **Winnt32.exe** based on the current operating system.

- Windows 2000 Server

  Only Windows NT 3.51 Server, Windows NT 4.0 Server, and Windows NT 4.0 Terminal Server can be upgraded to Windows 2000 Server. With any other operating system, you must run a clean installation.

- Windows 2000 Professional

  Only Windows 95, Windows 98, Windows NT 3.51 Workstation, and Windows NT 4.0 Workstation can be upgraded to Windows 2000 Professional. With any other operating system, you must run a clean installation.

- Upgrade procedures

  o   The Setup Wizard will prompt you with two choices:

      - Upgrade to Windows 2000 (recommended)

      - Install a new copy of Windows 2000 (clean install)

  o   If your boot drive is not currently formatted as NTFS, you will be prompted to upgrade the drive. This will convert the drive to NTFS.

  o   Setup will begin to follow its normal course. Setup will automatically:

      - Detect and install existing hardware devices.

      - Install networking components based on your current network configuration.

- Configure your network settings based on your current network configuration.

- Install server components if installing Windows 2000 Server.

- Install **Start** menu items.

- Register components.

- Save settings and remove any temporary files.

  o Windows 2000 will restart and will be ready to run.

- Dual-boot Setup

  o You can install Windows 2000 on a machine that already has Windows 98 on it. However, there are some points you should keep in mind.

    - Program settings

      Installation destination—You need to ensure that Windows 2000 is installed into a different folder than Windows 98. There are three reasons for this:

      o Registry structure

      o Hardware devices

      o Shared files

    - File systems

      Windows 98 supports only FAT and FAT32 partitions.

  o Steps for installing Windows 2000 on a Windows 98 machine

    - Ensure that the devices currently in your computer are supported by Windows 2000. Start Windows 98.

    - Launch the **Run** command from **Start**. Click on **Browse** and locate the directory that contains the Windows 2000 source files. Type the following:

      ```
      winnt /w
      ```

    - Install Windows 2000 into a different folder than Windows 98.

    - Reinstall any programs you plan to use under Windows 2000.

    - Restart your computer. You should be prompted to choose the operating system you would like to use.

o The information about dual booting is stored in the Boot.ini file at the root of the C: drive. This file is used by NTLDR to determine which operating system to boot. An operating system can be configured as the default from the Startup/Shutdown property page, which can be found on the **Advanced** tab in the Control Panel's System utility.

Course Reference Material

Manual

- Chapter 2
- Chapter 3

Digital Video

- Windows 98 Installation
- Windows 2000 Installation

NEXTSim

- Windows 95/98 Installation
  - o Upgrade Windows 95 to Windows 98

Challenge! Interactive

- Installation, Configuration, and Upgrading

Exam Criteria

2.3   Identify the basic system boot sequences and boot methods, including the steps to create an emergency boot disk with utilities installed for Windows 9x, Windows NT, and Windows 2000.

Points to Remember

Windows 95/98 Boot Process

- The Windows 9x boot process is as follows:
    - Power On Self Test (POST) will execute.
    - Master Boot Record (MBR) is loaded.
    - Io.sys is loaded.
    - Io.sys loads Himem.sys, Ifshlp.sys, and Setver.exe by default.
    - Msdos.sys is read.
    - Config.sys is processed, if present.
    - Autoexec.bat is processed, if present.
    - Win.com is executed.
        - The Windows Registry is processed.
        - Win.com loads Win.ini.
        - Win.com loads System.ini.
        - Virtual Device Drivers (VXDs) are loaded.
        - Windows kernel is loaded.
- Windows 95 safe mode
    - Windows 95 has a special diagnostic mode, safe mode, that allows you to fix problems that keep Windows from starting properly.
    - You may access the Windows 9x startup menu during bootup by pressing the *F8* key when you see "Starting Windows 9x..." appear on the screen.

o   If Windows 9x has problems booting, it will restart and display the following menu.

```
          Microsoft Windows 98 Startup Menu
          ==============================

1. Normal

2. Logged (\BOOTLOG.TXT)

3. Safe mode

4. Safe mode with network support

5. Step-by-step confirmation

6. Command prompt only

7. Safe mode command prompt only

Enter a choice:


F5=Safe mode Shift+F5=Command Prompt

Shift+F8=Step-by-step confirmation [N]
```

o   While in safe mode, Windows 9x uses these default settings:

- VGA monitor

- No network (unless in safe mode with network support)

- Microsoft mouse driver

- Minimum device drivers

- NTLDR

  NTLDR is the operating system loader. In a multiboot system, it will be used to start the other operating systems. It is a hidden, read-only system file that is located in the root of the boot drive.

- Boot.ini

  The Boot.ini files controls the ability to boot to more than one operating system on a single computer. The Boot.ini file is a hidden, read-only text file stored in the root of the system partition.

- Other Windows 2000 system files

  The table below outlines the boot files that are needed in the boot process.

File	Location	Boot Stage
NTLDR (hidden)	System partition root (C:\)	Preboot and boot
Boot.ini	System partition root	Boot
Bootsect.dos	System partition root	Boot
Ntdetect.com (hidden)	System partition root	Boot
Ntbootdd.sys (optional)	System partition root	Boot
Ntoskrnl.exe	Systemroot\System32	Kernel load
Hal.dll	Systemroot\System32	Kernel load
System	Systemroot\System32\Config Kernel initialization	Kernel initialization
Device drivers (*.sys)	Systemroot\System32\Drivers	Kernel initialization

- Windows 2000 boot process

  The Windows 2000 boot process can be broken down into five basic stages: preboot sequence, boot sequence, kernel load, kernel initialization, and logon stage.

  o Preboot/boot sequence

    - Power On Self Test (POST) will execute.

    - Master Boot Record (MBR) is loaded.

    - NTLDR file loads and is initalized.

    - The Boot.ini file is processed. The operating system selecting menu appears if dual booting is enabled in the Boot.ini file.

    - NTLDR runs Ntdetect.com, which scans the system hardware and returns the results back to NTLDR.

    - The boot configuration menu appears.

  o Kernel load

    - The Hardware Abstraction Layer (HAL) is loaded, which hides the physical hardware from applications.

    - The hardware portion of the Registry is loaded.

- o   Kernel initialization stage
  - The screen turns blue, and drivers are initialized and loaded.
  - **Winlogon.exe** is started.
- o   Logon stage

  Once the user logs on, the boot process is considered complete.
- Windows 2000 safe boot options

  You can start Windows 2000 safe mode by pressing *F8* when the **Boot** menu is displayed. After you press *F8*, the **Advanced Options** menu is displayed with the following options:
  - o   Safe Mode
  - o   Safe Mode with Networking
  - o   Safe Mode with Command Prompt
  - o   Enable Boot Logging
  - o   Enable VGA
  - o   Last Known Good Configuration
  - o   Directory Service Restore Mode
  - o   Debug Mode
  - o   Boot Normally
- Recovery Console
  - o   Recovery Console does not have a GUI.
  - o   Using the Administrator account and password, you can gain access to the Windows 2000 system files, run built-in diagnostic tools (Chkdsk, for example), and enable or disable services.
  - o   To run Recovery Console, you need a Microsoft Windows 2000 Installation CD. Start the computer with the CD-ROM in the drive or boot with disk 1 if you are using boot disks and follow the instructions on the screen. When the Welcome to Setup dialog box is displayed:
    1. Press *R* to choose the **Repair a Windows 2000 Installation** option.
    2. When the Windows 2000 Repair Options dialog box is displayed, press *C* to start Recovery Console.

3. The next dialog box displays a list of operating systems that are installed. Type the number of the Windows 2000 installation that you want to select.

4. Type the local Administrator password and press *ENTER.*

- Boot diskettes

Boot diskettes are used to start your system and get to a command prompt if you cannot or do not want to boot from the hard drive. Windows 9x startup disks and Windows 2000 emergency repair disks can also replace missing or damaged boot files.

- Windows 98 bootable diskette

To create a Windows 98 bootable diskette:

1. Insert a blank floppy disk into your floppy drive.

2. Click on the My Computer icon.

3. Right-click on the 3.5" Floppy A:\ icon and choose **Format.**

4. Choose **Copy system files only** if the disk is a blank formatted disk or **Copy system files** if the disk needs to be formatted.

5. Click on the **Start** button.

- Windows 98 Startup diskette

To create a Windows 9x Startup diskette:

1. Click on the **Start** button.

2. Choose **Settings.**

3. Click on Control Panel.

4. In the Control Panel window, double-click on the Add/Remove Programs icon.

5. Click on the **Startup Disk** tab.

6. Place a blank disk in the floppy drive, A:\.

7. Click on the **Create Disk** button and click on **OK.**

8. When prompted, remove the disk from the drive.

NOTE: *The process is the same for creating a Windows 95 boot diskette; however, no CD-ROM drivers are installed on the disk.*

- Windows 2000 Emergency Repair Disks (ERDs)
  - Windows 2000 ERDs will allow you to inspect the startup environment, verify the Windows 2000 system files, and inspect the boot sector. As an option, it can also back up Registry data.
  - To create an ERD:
    1. Select **Start | Programs | Accessories | System Tools | Backup**.
    2. Select the **Welcome** tab and click on the button next to **Emergency Repair Disk**.
    3. The Emergency Repair Disk window displays. Click on the box next to **Also backup the Registry to the repair directory**.
    4. Insert the floppy in the drive and click on **OK**.
- Windows NT Emergency Repair Disk (ERD)

  A Windows NT 4.0 ERD serves the same function as a Windows 2000 diskette but is created differently. To create or update a Windows NT ERD, use one of the following methods:
  - Type "rdisk /s" in the Open box.
  - Type "rdisk" in the Open box, then click on **Update Repair Info**.

Course Reference Material

Manual

- Chapter 2
- Chapter 4
  - Windows 95/98 Boot Process
  - Windows 2000 Boot Process
  - Boot Diskettes

Digital Video

- Windows 98 Installation
- Navigating Windows 98
- Navigating Windows 2000

NEXTSim

- Windows 95/98 Installation
  - o Upgrade Windows 95 to Windows 98

Challenge! Interactive

- Installation, Configuration, and Upgrading

Exam Criteria

2.4 Identify procedures for loading/adding and configuring application device drivers and the necessary software for certain devices.

Points to Remember

Device Drivers

Device drivers are the software that allows the operating system to talk with the hardware in a computer.

- Windows 95 drivers

  Windows 95 uses Virtual Device Drivers (VxDs) to manage system resources such as hardware devices and installed software. A VxD is a 32-bit, protected-mode driver that manages a system resource so that more than one application can use the resource at the same time.

- Windows 98 and 2000 drivers
  - o Windows 98 and 2000 use a new driver model that allows one driver to be written that can be used with both operating systems. Windows 98 retains backward compatibility with Windows 95 VxDs.
  - o All Windows 2000 drivers must adhere to the Win32 Driver Model (WDM) specification.

- Win32 Driver Model (WDM)

  WDM is a specification that Universal Serial Bus (USB), IEEE 1394, and Advanced Configuration and Power Interface (ACPI) are built on.

- Device class drivers

  Device class drivers enable the layers to communicate. The lower edge of a device class driver communicates with the device minidriver, and the upper edge is specific to the operating system. A device class driver:

  o   Contains class information that is not specific to a bus or hardware.

  o   Can dynamically load and unload.

  o   Exposes a single interface to multiple-client layers.

- Bus class drivers

  Bus class drivers enable communication between the hardware and the bus minidriver.

- Minidrivers

  o   Windows 95 already implemented minidrivers in network adapters and Small Computer System Interface (SCSI). With Windows 98, minidrivers are also utilized by USB, the IEEE 1394 bus, digital audio, DVD players, still imaging, and video capture.

  o   Minidrivers:

    - Can be used on both Windows 98 and Windows NT.

    - Can dynamically load and unload.

    - Function for hardware only.

    - Can expose many class interfaces.

- Installing device drivers

  o   When installing a new hardware device, be sure to follow any instructions provided by the device manufacturer.

  o   Some devices will automatically be detected and install drivers with little or no user intervention.

- Windows 98 Device Manager

  The Device Manager is accessed in Windows 98 by opening System from the Control Panel and selecting the **Device Manager** tab.

- Adding hardware

  When you attach a new hardware device to the computer before booting, Windows 98 will automatically detect the new hardware and install the appropriate device drivers for it, if necessary. If a new device is added while Windows 98 is running, the Add New Hardware Wizard should be used to identify the new hardware and load any necessary driver files.

- Removing hardware

  Hardware devices are removed from Windows 98 through the Device Manager utility. To remove a hardware device:

  1. Expand the type of hardware.

  2. Highlight the device.

  3. Click on **Remove** or right-click and select **Remove**.

- Updating device drivers

  o It is important to use the most up-to-date device drivers for your hardware.

  o The Update Device Driver Wizard enables a quick and appropriate device driver update. Click on **Update Driver** from an appropriate device Properties screen.

- Windows 2000 device drivers

  Windows 2000 has a few differences when working with drivers when compared to Windows 98.

  o User permissions

    You must be logged on as an Administrator (or a member of the Administrators group) to install device drivers.

  o Device Driver Signing

    Windows 2000 supports digitally signed drivers through Driver Signing. For a driver to be digitally signed, it must pass Windows Hardware Quality Labs (WHQL) certification tests.

- Updating Windows 2000 device drivers

  o There are two basic methods for updating device drivers. One method is to apply a service pack to the system. The other way is to apply individual device driver updates.

  o You can use the Device Manager to install an updated driver for a device. Display the device properties and click on the **Driver** tab, then click on **Update Driver**.

- Configuration settings

  The following four basic configuration settings apply to most adapter cards:

  o Interrupt Request (IRQ) line

  o I/O address

  o Memory (ROM BIOS)

  o Direct Memory Access (DMA)

- Hardware Compatibility List (HCL)

  The HCL is a list of hardware that has been tested and verified as compatible with Windows 2000.

- Plug and Play device management

  In most cases, Windows 2000 recognizes and installs Plug and Play hardware devices automatically.

- Legacy device management

  o If Windows 2000 doesn't recognize the device automatically, or if the Found New Hardware Wizard is unable to properly install the device, you will likely need to use the Add/Remove Hardware Wizard.

  o Uninstalling a legacy device is typically a two-step process.

    1. Let Windows 2000 know you are uninstalling the device. You can do this through either the Add/Remove Hardware utility or the Device Manager Snap-in.

    2. Physically remove the device.

Windows 98 Printer Management

- Print subsystem organization

  o The printer driver architecture uses a multithreaded, pre-emptive architecture.

  o The pre-emptive multitasking printing architecture offers:

    - Increased printing performance

    - Smooth background printing

    - Quick return to the sending application

  o The print subsystem contains the following components:

    - GDI

    - Raw or enhanced metafile (EMF) formatted files

    - Print spooler

    - Print processor

- Spooling and despooling
  - *Spooling* occurs when the print job is stored in an area of memory called the buffer or on the hard disk. *Despooling* takes the spooled data and sends it to the printer.
  - To configure spool settings:
    1. Launch the Printers dialog from the Control Panel or select **Printers** from the **Start | Settings** menu.
    2. Right-click on the bi-directional printer and select **Properties**.
    3. Display the **Details** tab and click on **Spool Settings**.
- Spooled files

  Spooled files are added to the hidden Windows\Spool\Printers directory.
- Bidirectional printing
  - Bidirectional printing is a parallel type of communication.
  - The following components are required for bidirectional printing:
    - A bidirectional printer
    - An IEEE 1284-compliant cable
    - A bidirectional parallel port set to bidirectional or PS/2 mode
- Extended Capabilities Port (ECP)
  - ECP devices offer high-speed printing by improving the input/output performance.
  - The following components are required to take full advantage of an ECP port:
    - An IEEE 1284-compliant cable
    - An ECP printer
- Fonts
  - Windows 98 provides four kinds of fonts:
    - TrueType
    - OpenType (new to Windows 98 and 2000)
    - Raster
    - Vector

o   Windows 98 uses the following rules to determine a matching font:

- TrueType or OpenType fonts are rendered by TrueType, then sent to the display or printer.

- With fonts other than TrueType or OpenType, the font mapping table is used to determine the most appropriate device font to use.

o   Fonts can be installed in many ways on a Windows 98 computer. These include:

- During Windows 98 Setup, Screen, TrueType, and OpenType fonts are installed

- During some applications' Setup process

- From a disk, network, or other location

- Using the printer's Properties dialog

- Printing from MS-DOS applications

o   Print spooling for MS-DOS applications only works with LPTx (parallel) ports.

o   MS-DOS is spooled by default but is disabled automatically when:

- A port is redirected to a network printer, overriding the MS-DOS print job spool setting.

- Windows 98 is run in MS-DOS mode.

- Installing a network printer

    A network printer can be installed on your local computer using Network Neighborhood or the Add Printer Wizard.

- Using Point and Print

    Point and Print allows a network printer to be installed locally without requiring any action from the user. Both NetWare and Windows NT 4.0 networks have Point and Print capabilities.

- Deferred Printing

    Deferred Printing is enabled by setting a network printer to work offline or a local printer to pause printing.

- HP JetAdmin

    The Hewlett-Packard JetAdmin application allows you to control the setup and configuration of HP printers that are connected to an HP JetDirect print server.

Microsoft Windows Application Support

Windows 95, 98, and 2000 all provide MS-DOS and 16-bit Windows application support in addition to their support for 32-bit applications. Support is provided through the Win32 Application Programming Interface (API).

- Support for MS-DOS applications
  - MS-DOS-based applications can run inside Windows 98 or from an MS-DOS window.
  - Through the use of Virtual Device Drivers (VxDs), each MS-DOS application receives access to hardware components.
- Virtual Machines (VMs)
  - A VM consists of a virtual address space in physical or virtual memory, processor registers, and privileges.
  - The System Virtual Machine contains:
    - Base system components (GDI, USER, kernel)
    - Memory address space shared by all Windows 16-bit applications
    - Individual memory address spaces for each Windows 32-bit application
    - A separate MS-DOS VM for each MS-DOS application
- PIF files
  - Each application has an application information file, or PIF file.
  - The system looks for an application's PIF file in the following order:
    - The directory where the executable file is located
    - The Windows PIF directory
    - The Autoexec.bat file
    - The Apps.inf file for a match
    - A default PIF file from the application or from the Apps.inf file
      - If Windows 98 was installed over Windows 3.1, it uses the _default.pif file.
      - The _default.pif file can be created by copying Dosprmpt.pif to _default.pif.

- Memory available to MS-DOS applications

  Windows 98 makes much more conventional memory available to your MS-DOS applications by replacing 16-bit real-mode drivers with 32-bit protected-mode drivers for the following:

  o Share.exe

  o Mouse.com

  o Smartdrv.ext

  o Mscdex.exe

  o Drvspace.sys

- 16-bit applications

  Some facts to remember about Win16-based applications include:

  o The operating system provides the same system resources to both Win32-based and Win16-based applications.

  o Win16-based applications cannot utilize pre-emptive multitasking or long filename support.

  o Win16-based applications share memory address space in the System VM, a common input queue, and a common message queue.

  o Win16-based processes are scheduled cooperatively.

  o Win16-based applications make use of 32-bit print and communications subsystems.

- 32-bit applications

  Advantages of Win32-based applications include:

  o Pre-emptive multitasking

  o Long filename support

  o Memory protection

  o Separate message queue for each application

- Multitasking

  There are two distinct ways of handling how multiple applications run at the same time.

  o Cooperative multitasking

  o Pre-emptive multitasking

- Resource sharing

    Through the use of File and Printer Sharing for Microsoft Networks, you can share resources on a Windows 98 computer to other Windows-family computers on the network.

- User-level security

    o   With user-level security, a security provider such as a Windows NT PDC authenticates a user.

    o   All of the following must be installed to implement user-level security:

    - User-level access control enabled

    - Client for Microsoft Networks installed and configured to Client for Microsoft Networks Logon

    - File and Printer Sharing for Microsoft Networks service installed

- Accessing shared user-level resources

    In order to gain access to a resource protected with user-level security sharing, a user must have logged on to the domain with the appropriate name and been granted the appropriate access to the resource.

- Sharing a folder

    A folder is shared from the Sharing properties page of the folder's Properties window.

- Share-level permissions

    o   Share permissions are checked only when a user attempts to access a shared resource across a network.

    o   By default, the Everyone group is given Full Control access to a shared folder.

- Combining Share and NT File System (NTFS) permissions

    When a folder on an NTFS volume is shared, a user requesting access to a resource across the network must pass access checks at both the share level and the NTFS permissions level.

- Sharing a folder with multiple share names

    You can associate multiple share names with a single folder by clicking on **New Share**. A dialog will be displayed, prompting you for information about the new share.

- Removing shares

  A share is removed simply by clicking on the **Do not share this folder** option on the Sharing properties page and applying the change.

- Persistent connections

  Drive letters can also be assigned to another computer's shared resource. This is done by mapping a network drive to the path of the resource on another computer.

Course Reference Material

Manual

- Chapter 7
  - o Device Drivers
  - o Windows 2000 Device Drivers
  - o Windows 98 Printer Management
- Chapter 8
  - o Microsoft Windows Application Support
  - o 16-Bit and 32-Bit Windows Applications
- Chapter 10
  - o Resource Sharing

NEXTSim

- Hardware Management
  - o Configure and Troubleshoot an I/O Device
  - o Configure Printing
- Software Management
  - o Configure a DOS-based Application

Challenge! Interactive

- Installation, Configuration, and Upgrading

DOMAIN 3.0 DIAGNOSING AND TROUBLESHOOTING

Exam Criteria

3.1 Recognize and interpret the meaning of common error codes and startup messages from the boot sequence and identify steps to correct the problems.

Points to Remember

Troubleshooting Windows

- Troubleshooting bad or missing files

  When starting Windows 9x, you may receive a message that there is a bad or missing file. If this is the case, ensure that the entry in the Config.sys file (or other Startup file referenced by the error message) has the correct syntax. Also, check to ensure that the file is indeed on your system and located in the correct directory. You should also make sure the file that is attempting to load is the right version and not corrupt.

- Bad or missing command interpreter

  An example of a bad or missing file is the Bad or Missing Command Interpreter error. This error occurs when the Command.com file is corrupted or missing and will prevent Windows 9x from starting.

- VFAT Initialization error

  The VFAT Initialization error can be caused by a number of situations. What follows are two of the most common causes:

  o Ifshlp.sys file is missing from the Windows folder.

  o Config.sys is missing the Ifshlp.sys statement.

- Device driver problems

  If you install a third-party Windows 3.x version of a device driver in Windows 9x, the driver may cause Windows 9x to not start properly. If this is the case, restart in safe mode, remove all entries in System.ini that were added by this installation, delete the device in Device Manager, shut down and restart Windows 9x, and use the Add New Hardware Wizard to reinstall the device.

- Windows safe mode operations
  - o Windows has a special diagnostic mode, safe mode, that allows you to get to the Windows desktop even when you have problems that keep Windows from starting properly. Frequently, incorrect network, video, or other hardware drivers cause these types of problems.
  - o You may access the Windows 9x Startup menu during bootup by pressing the *CONTROL* or *F8* key when the "Starting Windows 95" or "Starting Windows 98" message appears on the screen.

Troubleshooting Startup Problems in Windows 98

- System File Checker

Sometimes when an application is installed, it may overwrite important shared files, such as ActiveX controls or dynamic-link libraries. In addition, users may accidentally delete important files, or disk problems may corrupt vital system files. The System File Checker (Sfc.exe in \Windows\System) is used to scan for problems like these.

- Automatic Skip Driver (ASD) agent
  - o The ASD (Asd.exe) agent runs automatically when the computer boots to determine if hardware device drivers or other operations have failed.
  - o Following are several operations that can cause ASD to run:
    - Using a device
    - Device enumeration
    - PnP Basic Input/Output System (BIOS)
    - Peripheral Component Interconnect (PCI) BIOS
    - PCI Interrupt Request (IRQ) routing table from a PCI BIOS 2.1 call
    - Video Electronics Standards Association (VESA) BIOS
    - Video BIOS post
    - Video BIOS post after standby
    - Address space mapping
    - Power state configuration of a graphics device

- Version Conflict Manager (VCM)

  If an application has installed shared files on a computer that has a higher file version number than the version of the file installed by Window 98, Windows 98 will automatically move the later version of the file to the Windows\VCM directory and install the older source file during the Windows 98 Setup Copying Files stage.

- System Configuration utility

  The System Configuration utility (Msconfig.exe in \Windows\System) is used to troubleshoot problems by eliminating the items that are working properly.

- Event Viewer

  Device driver and service failures will be recorded in the System log. When you receive a message that a service or device driver has failed, the System log is a good place to start troubleshooting.

- Device Manager

  The Device Manager lets you quickly identify failing devices. When a device failure is detected, the Device Manager will automatically expand the device category and identify the failing device with an exclamation point.

- Failing drives

  o *Transient* errors are intermittent or one-time errors that occur in passing, and you never (or at least seldom) see them again. Transient errors can come from any number of sources, such as static discharge, momentary timing conflicts, a power sag or surge, or a drive that just didn't respond quickly enough to a request. You will probably never know exactly what happened or why, and in most cases, there is no reason to be concerned about it. Clear the error and watch for it to reoccur.

  o *Hard* errors are usually easy to detect because the drive (or drive controller) simply doesn't work. You need to repair or replace the failing component, then correct any data errors caused by the condition.

Course Reference Material

Manual

- Chapter 4
  - o Windows 2000 System Files
- Chapter 7
  - o Memory Fundamentals
  - o Windows 98 Memory Management
  - o Device Drivers
- Chapter 8
  - o Windows Error Messages
- Chapter 12

Digital Video

- Navigating Windows 98
- Navigating Windows 2000
- Windows 98 Troubleshooting Tools
- Windows 2000 Troubleshooting Tools

NEXTSim

- Hardware Management
  - o Configure and Troubleshoot an I/O Device
- Software Management
  - o Modify Dr. Watson Options in Windows 2000
- Troubleshooting Windows
  - o Use System Configuration Utility and Sysedit
  - o Create and Configure an Alert Object
  - o Use the Event Viewer

Challenge! Interactive

- Diagnosing and Troubleshooting

Exam Criteria

3.2   Recognize common problems and determine how to resolve them.

Points to Remember

Windows 95 and 98 Errors

- Nonresponding applications

  Applications can fail in two ways: either an application can violate system integrity by performing a prohibited command or an application can lock up by failing to respond to messages sent to it from the operating system.

- Windows protection errors

  A Windows protection error occurs when there is a problem loading or unloading a Virtual Device Driver (VxD).

- Illegal operations

  The term illegal operation is a generic error message. If you get a message saying that a program has performed an illegal operation, you will need to click on the **Details** button to see the full error message.

- General Protection Faults (GPFs)

  What causes these errors is when a program sends the system a command that is invalid or otherwise cannot be processed. GPFs can be caused by data corruption or conflicts between two programs that are accessing the processor simultaneously.

- Invalid page faults

  Invalid page faults occur when one program running on a computer tries to access memory that another program has already reserved for itself.

- System lockups

  Typically, system lockups are caused by the same things as general protection faults and invalid page faults, but they create a state in which the system can no longer respond and an error message cannot be displayed.

- Fatal exception errors

  Exceptions are generated by the computer's processor. A fatal exception means the exception cannot be handled by the program or Windows, and thus, the program will not be able to continue to run.

- Troubleshooting error messages

  When troubleshooting error messages, you should determine:
  - What module or program did the error occur in?
  - What was the user doing at the time the error occurred?
  - Is the problem reproducible, or does it occur at random?
  - Have there been any recent changes made to the system?
  - Does the problem occur only in the current application or in other applications as well?
  - Are there specific, known issues about the application that describe your problem?
  - Does the problem occur only at a particular time, such as while printing?

- Windows 2000 error messages

  When Windows 2000 detects an error that it cannot recover from, it generates an error message. There are two types of system messages generated by Windows 2000: stop messages and hardware malfunction messages.

- Dr. Watson

  Dr. Watson is used to detail GPFs and what software was involved when an error occurs.

Virus Prevention

A virus is a software program that has the ability to reproduce by modifying other programs or by duplicating itself. It is a parasitic program written intentionally to enter a computer without the user's permission or knowledge.

- Types of viruses

  Virus are classified by the ways they infect computer systems:
  - Program viruses
  - Boot sector viruses
  - Macro viruses

- Other malicious programs

  Some malicious programs cannot be classified as viruses because they either do not self-replicate or they do not infect other programs. Examples include:
  - Trojans
  - Worms

- Where do they come from?

They are specifically written to invade your system and duplicate themselves.

- How do they enter systems?

Quite simply, viruses enter your systems because you are not careful in avoiding them. Unsafe computing practices, such as running programs from unknown sources, allowing unlimited access, and so on, invite infection. Viruses can arrive by e-mail attachments, by floppy disk, or with software.

- What do they do?

The results depend on the virus. Some are destructive, but most are benign. They tend to infect boot sectors and executables (COM, EXE, and BAT files). They may corrupt data or program files, corrupt the boot sector, format hard or floppy disks, corrupt the FAT, or just display odd messages on the screen.

- What are some common specialized viruses?

Not so long ago, viruses that infected boot sectors were the most common. Today, specialized viruses that infect Microsoft Word and Microsoft Excel files have become the most common type. Since these viruses use the macro language of the specific application to spread, they are known as *macro viruses*.

- Word macro viruses

These viruses use the WordBasic macro language to infect and replicate in and among Microsoft Word documents and templates.

- Excel macro viruses

When an infected spreadsheet is first opened on a system, the Auto_Open macro is automatically run by Excel, which in turn runs the Check_Files macro. This happens each time a worksheet is activated.

- Master Boot Record (MBR) viruses

MBR viruses spread by floppy disk. If an infected floppy is left in the drive when the machine is turned off and then on again, the machine is infected because it reads the boot sectors of the floppy expecting to find the operating system there. The virus then copies itself to the boot record of the hard drive. Once the hard drive is infected, the boot virus may replicate itself onto all of the floppies that are accessed by the computer until the virus is removed.

- How do you prevent infections?

  o The best way to prevent a virus is to never allow anything to be copied to the system or run any unchecked software. If this is not practical (and it probably isn't), you need to practice safe computing.

  o Install virus prevention software.

  o Do not run software from unknown or unreliable sources.

  o Be on the alert for viruses downloaded via Internet e-mail attachments.

  o Do not let employees bring software from home.

  o Test software downloaded from bulletin board systems and the Internet on a test system, not a production system.

  o Do not share diskettes between computers.

  o Do not boot a computer with a startup diskette that has been used in another computer.

  o Write-protect all boot diskettes.

  o Remove diskettes from drives immediately after use.

  o Run a virus detection program on a regular basis or when infection is suspected.

  o Back up data and program files on a regular basis and rotate backup media.

  o Be diligent about your own materials; maintenance personnel are a major source of infections because they take the same software tool kit from site to site.

- Anti-viral programs

  There are many anti-viral programs available. You can classify the programs by their function.

  o Maintenance (viral scan)

     These are programs that can be run periodically to check for viral infection but do not provide constant protection.

  o Preventive

     Your best bet is to keep the infection from ever happening. Install anti-virus software that will run as a service in the background, monitoring for any virus-like activities. To keep the anti-virus software effective, you must also update the signature files regularly.

- Virus recovery

  If you determine the type of infection you have, tailor your recovery to the virus type:

  o   Boot sector

      Boot from a Windows 98 Startup disk or a Windows 2000 Emergency Repair Disk and rewrite the boot sector.

  o   Executable files

      Boot from a floppy, delete all infected files, and recover from the distribution diskettes or recover from backups.

  o   FAT or directory tables

      Run a low-level format and recover from backups.

Printer Management and Troubleshooting

- Windows 98 Print Troubleshooter

  The primary print troubleshooting device provided by Windows 98 is the Print Troubleshooter. It is an interactive troubleshooter. It proceeds with additional information and questions in response to your answers.

- Problems during printer installation

  There are several potential problems that can occur during printer installation. Following are a few of them and suggestions for fixing them.

  o   The list of manufacturers and printers is blank.

      The list of printers that are displayed in the Add Printer Wizard come from the Prtupd.inf file that is located in the Windows INF directory. Verify that the file is available.

  o   The necessary printer driver files cannot be found.

      When the Add Printer Wizard cannot find or access the necessary printer driver files, you are prompted to enter a path to the printer files. Browse to the source directory or installation media where the drivers are located. If it will not accept the drivers, make sure that you have the correct drivers for the printer that you are installing.

  o   The necessary printer files did not copy properly.

      If an error occurs during the transfer of the necessary printer driver files, the error is displayed on the screen. You should verify that both the source media and your computer are error free and then add the printer again.

- Installation printer test

    During installation of a printer, you can send a test page to the printer to confirm that the printer printed the test page properly.

- Printers.txt file

    There is a Windows 98 printer information file called Printers.txt located in the Windows folder. It provides the most up-to-date information regarding specific printer models and printing problems.

- Printing from Windows 9x applications

    o   If you are unable to print from a Windows application, you may need to change your bidirectional printing settings.

    o   If you have problems printing clear documents or graphics in Windows 95, you may do one of two options:

    - Use the Generic/Text Only printer driver.

    - Update your driver.

- Too slow

    By clicking on **Spool Settings** on the **Details** tab, you can set the printer to print after the first page has been spooled.

- Local printer problems

    o   If the source of the problem still is not apparent, you can try to print to the LPT1.dos port.

    o   Some other steps to try when troubleshooting local printer problems include:

    - Clear the print queue.

    - Print a test page.

    - Check the paper.

    - Check to see if the printer is online.

- Network printer problems

    If users are having trouble printing to a network printer, it could be that the network is down.

- Printer garbage

    First, cycle power to the printer. If you are still receiving garbled images or text when trying to print, start the computer in safe mode.

Troubleshooting Modems and Remote Access

- Troubleshooting modem installation

  A modem may not be detected because:

  - The modem may not be connected properly to the computer.
  - The COM port may be assigned to another device.
  - The modem is already installed.
  - The COM port may not be configured properly.
  - The Add New Hardware utility can be used to detect and install the COM port.
  - The COM port's IRQ setting is in conflict with an IRQ setting of another device.

- Modem diagnostic tool

  The primary troubleshooting tool for modems is located on the **Diagnostics** tab of the Modems Properties dialog.

- Dial-up Networking problems

  When a user tries to use a Dial-up Networking connection but has trouble connecting, there could be several problems:

  - The modem is dialing, but no connection is made.
  - The user is using an internal modem.
  - The user is using an external modem.
  - The user gets disconnected.

- Windows 98 remote administration tools

  The remote administration tools included with Windows 98 are:

  - Registry Editor (Regedit.exe)
  - System Monitor (Sysmon.exe)
  - System Policy Editor (Poledit.exe)
  - Net Watcher (Netwatch.exe)

- Remote Registry Editor

  - The Registry Editor (Regedit.exe) can be used to connect to local and remote registries.
  - Any changes that are made to the remote Registry are automatically enabled.

- System Monitor

  The System Monitor enables the administrator to monitor a local or remote computer's performance related to many variables.

- System Policy Editor

  System Policy Editor with remote administration enables a connection to a remote computer. The administrator can then define or update user and system policies for the remote user.

- Net Watcher

  Net Watcher allows you to view, access, and create shared resources on a remote computer.

Questioning Skills

Questioning skills are one of your most important troubleshooting tools. Effective questioning techniques, coupled with good listening habits, will enable you to resolve problems more quickly by focusing and redirecting conversations with your customer.

- Troubleshooting basics

  There are some general guidelines that apply to nearly any type of problem you are going to encounter. These include the following:

  o Define the problem.

  o Look for obvious causes and solutions.

  o Use available tools.

  o Change one thing at a time.

  o Document everything.

- Close-ended questioning techniques

  A close-ended question is very different than an open-ended question. In this type of question, you will pose your question as more of a statement, then ask for a yes or no confirmation, or you will ask a question that has a simple yes or no answer.

- Open-ended questioning techniques

  An open-ended question is one that, when asked, gives your customer the unlimited freedom to answer as he/she wishes.

Course Reference Material

Manual

- Chapter 4
    - Windows 95/98 System Files
    - Windows 2000 System Files
- Chapter 5
    - Hard Drive Optimization
- Chapter 8
    - Windows Error Messages
    - Virus Prevention
- Chapter 12

Digital Video

- Navigating Windows 98
- Navigating Windows 2000
- Windows 98 Troubleshooting Tools
- Windows 2000 Troubleshooting Tools

NEXTSim

- Windows 98 Disk and File Management
    - Run System Utilities for Hard Disk Management
- Software Management
    - Modify Dr. Watson Options in Windows 2000
- Troubleshooting Windows
    - Create and Configure an Alert Object
    - Use the Event Viewer

Challenge! Interactive

- Diagnosing and Troubleshooting

DOMAIN 4.0 NETWORKS

Exam Criteria

4.1   Identify the networking capabilities of Windows, including procedures for connecting to the network.

Points to Remember

Network Terms and Concepts

- Network

  In its simplest terms, a network is a set of computers and other devices connected in a manner that allows them to communicate.

- Subnetwork

  A subnetwork, like its name implies, is a subdivided portion of a network.

- Local Area Network (LAN)

  In a LAN configuration, all of the systems are locally connected.

- Wide Area Network (WAN)

  By classic definition, a LAN becomes a WAN when a public carrier is used to make one or more links.

- About remote access

  Remote access generally refers to a dial-in connection to a network or to a single server.

- Enterprise networking

  Generally, enterprise is an all-encompassing term including your systems, other networking devices, and all of your applications.

- Network addresses
  - Media Access Control (MAC) address

    The MAC address uniquely identifies each network adapter and, through the network adapter, the computer.

  - Computer name

    Computer names are used to provide a human-friendly way of identifying computers on the network.

- o   Host/system address

    In addition to the MAC address coded on the network adapter card, some protocols also use system addresses. A host address is a numeric value that uniquely identifies a computer as part of a network.

- o   Network address

    A computer's full address includes both its network address and host address.

- Cable plant

    The cable plant traditionally refers to the wires running between network systems.

- Low-level protocols

    Low-level protocols describe how systems communicate at the most basic level.

- Connectivity devices

    - o   Repeater
    - o   Hub
    - o   Switch
    - o   Bridge
    - o   Router
    - o   Gateway

Network Components

- Clients

    - o   Windows 98 includes these 32-bit clients:
        - Client for Microsoft Networks
        - Client for NetWare Networks
        - Microsoft Family Logon
    - o   Windows 98 also includes these real-mode networking clients:
        - Banyan DOS/Windows 3.1 client
        - FTP Software NFS client (InterDrive 95)
        - Novell NetWare [Workstation Shell 3.x (NETX)]
        - Novell NetWare [Workstation Shell 4.0 and above (VLM)]

- Protocols

  o A protocol is a set of strict rules that govern the exchange of information between networked computers.

  o Protocols included with Windows 98 are listed in the following table.

Manufacturer	Network Protocol
Banyan	Banyan VINES Ethernet Protocol Banyan VINES Token Ring Protocol
IBM	Existing IBM DLC Protocol
Microsoft	ATM Call Manager ATM Emulated LAN ATM LAN Emulation Client Fast Infrared Protocol IPX/SPX-compatible Protocol Microsoft 32-bit DLC Microsoft DLC NetBEUI TCP/IP
Novell	Novell IPX ODI Protocol

- Services

  A Windows 98 service allows the computer to share files, printers, and other resources such as tape backup with other computers on a network. Windows 98 includes two main types of services:

  o Hewlett-Packard

    The Hewlett-Packard (HP) options involve JetAdmin, which is a service that allows printing involving HP printers that are directly attached to the network.

  o Microsoft

    Microsoft options include the following:

    - File and Printer Sharing for Microsoft Networks
    - File and Printer Sharing for NetWare Networks
    - Service for NetWare Directory Services

- Resource sharing

  Through the use of File and Printer Sharing for Microsoft Networks, you can share resources on a Windows 98 computer to other Windows-family computers on the network.

- User-level security
  - o With user-level security, a security provider such as a Windows NT PDC authenticates a user.
  - o All of the following must be installed to implement user-level security:
    - User-level access control enabled
    - Client for Microsoft Networks installed and configured to Client for Microsoft Networks Logon
    - File and Printer Sharing for Microsoft Networks service installed
- Accessing shared user-level resources

  In order to gain access to a resource protected with user-level security sharing, a user must have logged on to the domain with the appropriate name and been granted the appropriate access to the resource.

- Sharing a folder

  A folder is shared from the Sharing properties page of the folder's Properties window.

- Share-level permissions
  - o Share permissions are checked only when a user attempts to access a shared resource across a network.
  - o By default, the Everyone group is given Full Control access to a shared folder.
- Combining Share and NT File System (NTFS) permissions

  When a folder on an NTFS volume is shared, a user requesting access to a resource across the network must pass access checks at both the share level and the NTFS permissions level.

- Sharing a folder with multiple share names

  You can associate multiple share names with a single folder by clicking on **New Share.** A dialog will be displayed, prompting you for information about the new share.

- Removing shares

  A share is removed simply by clicking on the **Do not share this folder** option on the Sharing properties page and applying the change.

- Persistent connections

  Drive letters can also be assigned to another computer's shared resource. This is done by mapping a network drive to the path of the resource on another computer.

Course Reference Material

Manual

- Chapter 9
- Chapter 10
- Chapter 11

NEXTSim

- Windows 98 LAN Management
  - Network and Share Resources on Windows 98
  - Share Folders with a NetWare Network
- Internet Technologies
  - Create a Dial-up Networking Connection in Windows 98
  - Install the Internet Connection Sharing Utility in Windows 98
  - Configure or Troubleshoot a Modem
  - Connect to the Internet Using Dial-up Networking

Challenge! Interactive

- Networks

Exam Criteria

4.2   Identify concepts and capabilities relating to the Internet and basic procedures for setting up a system for Internet access.

Points to Remember

- NetBEUI
  - o   Use NetBEUI:
    - On small LANs with no routing requirements
    - In environments where NetBEUI is already in use, such as Microsoft LAN Manager, Windows for Workgroups peer networks, Windows NT Server, and other networks
  - o   NetBEUI provides the following types of data traffic:
    - Connectionless
    - Connection-oriented
- IPX/SPX

  IPX/SPX protocol (nwlink.vxd) supports a Novell NetWare client, Windows NT server network, or a combination of the two.

- Transmission Control Protocal/Internet Protocol (TCP/IP)

  Microsoft TCP/IP allows computers with various operating systems and configurations to communicate over diverse networks.

- IP addressing
  - o   There are two types of IP addresses:
    - Globally unique IP addresses
    - Private IP addresses
  - o   There are two ways to configure an address:
    - Dynamic IP addressing
    - Static IP addressing
  - o   An IP address is a 32-bit address, written as four octets (bytes) separated by periods.

- Subnetting
  - o Each network must have its own network address.
  - o Networks are linked by routers.
  - o The subnet mask identifies the network and host addresses.
  - o An assigned address class, using the default subnet mask, provides a single network address.
- Domain Name System (DNS)
  - o DNS maps names statically, and WINS maps names dynamically.
  - o DNS uses a domain namespace where WINS uses a flat namespace (all on one domain).
- Windows Internet Name Service (WINS)

  WINS runs on Windows NT Server. It is a database that registers and resolves computer (NetBIOS) names to IP addresses in a routed or nonrouted network.

The Internet

- The Internet was developed in the late 1960s as a military project sponsored by the U.S. Defense Department called Advanced Research Projects Agency Network (ARPANET).
- World Wide Web
  - o The World Wide Web is the most visible and widely used portion of the Internet. The World Wide Web is an intricate maze of interconnected servers that support specially formatted documents called Web pages.
  - o No single agency owns or controls the Internet. The U.S. government ceased federal funding in 1995. For practical purposes, the Internet is funded primarily by commercial interests.
- Open standards

  One of the strengths of the Internet is that a specific type of computer is not required to join the Internet: IBM PC compatibles, Macintosh, UNIX-based machines, minicomputers, IBM mainframes, Windows NT servers, and Cray supercomputers are all part of the Internet.

- Intranets

  Intranets use the same technologies as the Internet but are either not connected to the Internet at all or have tightly controlled access for authorized users only.

- Extranets

  Many organizations found that certain key customers needed to gain access to portions of their internal information systems as a value-added customer service. Extranets extend the intranet architecture to allow designated external clients to access secure internal information sources.

- Firewalls

  Firewalls are an extra layer of security built in to routers to protect private networks from external intruders.

- Uniform Resource Locator (URL)

  o Every place on the Web has a unique address called a URL. A URL is a standard way of expressing a Web address and its data type. A URL can point to a file, Web site, page, or just about anything on the Internet.

  o The URL has a standard format that defines the precise destination address.

Service	Host Computer	Directory Path	File
http://	www.wavetech.com/	schedule/	resource.html

- Hypertext Transfer Protocol (HTTP)

  HTTP is the protocol that governs the transfer of HTML documents over the Web.

- Hypertext Markup Language (HTML)

  HTML is the coding language of the World Wide Web that tells browsers how to display a document's text, hyperlinks, graphics, and attached media.

- File Transfer Protocol (FTP)

  FTP is a commonly used method of moving files between two systems on the Internet.

- Usenet (newsgroups)

  Usenet is a means of facilitating discussion groups or forums.

- Multipurpose Internet Mail Extensions (MIME)

  MIME is more of a standard than a protocol. Used by e-mail applications, it is a method for sending files back and forth between computers through e-mail.

- Web browsers

  Web browsers are full-featured software packages that offer transparent client access to Web search engines, FTP servers, newsgroups, Telnet services, and Gopher clients. The two most popular browsers are Netscape Navigator and Microsoft Internet Explorer. Netscape Navigator is available as a free download. Internet Explorer is an integral part of the Microsoft Windows operating systems, and free updates are available from the Microsoft Internet site.

Internet Service Providers (ISPs)

- ISPs maintain a network that is linked to the Internet via a dedicated communication line, usually a high-speed T1, T3, or OC3 line. Using a modem, you dial up the service provider. The ISP's computers then connect you to the Internet, typically for a set monthly fee.

- Configuring an Internet dial-up connection in Windows 98

  - To use Dial-up Networking to connect to the Internet, you need the following:

    - One or more compatible modems

    - An installed network client

    - An installed dial-up adapter

    - TCP/IP protocol linked to the dial-up adapter

    - A valid dial-up Internet Point-to-Point Protocol (PPP) account

  - In addition to this, you need to obtain the following information from your ISP:

    - The dial-up telephone number

    - The IP addresses for the primary and secondary DNS servers

  - To configure a dial-up networking connection:

    1. Open the Dial-up Networking object within My Computer.

    2. Double-click on the Make New Connection icon.

- Configuring an Internet dial-up connection in Windows 2000
    - Configuring a dial-up connection in Windows 2000 is not much different than in Windows 98. You will need the same information from your ISP. You will also need:
        - One or more compatible modems
        - An installed network client
        - An installed dial-up adapter
        - TCP/IP protocol linked to the dial-up adapter
        - A valid dial-up Internet PPP account
        - The dial-up telephone number
    - To set up a Dial-up Networking connection in Windows 2000:
        1. Open the Network and Dial-up Networking objects within the Control Panel.
        2. Double-click on the Make New Connection icon.

Course Reference Material

Manual

- Chapter 9
- Chapter 11

NEXTSim

- Windows 98 LAN Management
    - Network a Windows 98 Computer to a NetWare Server
    - Network a Windows 98 Computer to a Windows NT Server
- Internet Technologies
    - Create a Dial-up Networking Connection in Windows 98
    - Install the Internet Connection Sharing Utility in Windows 98
    - Connect to the Internet Using Dial-up Networking

Challenge! Interactive

- Networks